Empowering Learning

Transforming Education Through Digital Tools and Platforms

Del Long

Empowering Learning

Chapter 1: Introduction to Educational Technology

The History and Evolution of EdTech

The landscape of education has undergone a profound transformation over the years, shaped by technological advancements that have redefined how knowledge is imparted and acquired. This evolution can be traced back to ancient times, where the use of rudimentary tools like papyrus and chalkboards began to lay the groundwork for a more structured approach to teaching. As societies evolved, so too did their educational practices, leading to the rich tapestry of educational technology we see today.

In the early 20th century, the introduction of radio and television marked a significant turning point. These mediums allowed educators to reach wider audiences, transcending geographical boundaries. Imagine a teacher in a classroom in the Midwest broadcasting lessons to students across the country. The ability to share knowledge in this way was revolutionary, yet it was just a precursor to the digital age that awaited.

The true explosion of educational technology began with the advent of computers in the 1980s. Schools began to integrate computers into their curricula, introducing students to basic programming and computer literacy. This period saw the rise of software designed specifically for educational purposes, such as drill-and-practice applications that reinforced fundamental skills in subjects like math and reading. However, the potential of these tools was often underutilized, as many educators were not adequately trained to incorporate technology into their teaching practices.

The 1990s heralded the internet's arrival in classrooms, fundamentally altering the educational landscape. Suddenly, vast resources were available at the fingertips of both students and educators. Online databases, academic journals, and educational websites became indispensable tools for research and learning. Email communication facilitated collaboration between teachers and students, fostering a sense of community that transcended physical spaces. As a result, traditional teaching methods began to shift towards more interactive and student-centered approaches.

The early 2000s saw the emergence of Learning Management Systems (LMS), which revolutionized the way educational content was delivered. Platforms like Blackboard and Moodle allowed educators to design and manage courses online, enabling a blended learning environment that combined face-to-face instruction with online resources. This hybrid model catered to diverse learning styles and provided students with greater flexibility in their studies. The LMS era also ushered in the concept of flipped classrooms, where students engage with instructional content at home and apply their knowledge in class, fostering deeper understanding and critical thinking.

As technology continued to advance, the rise of mobile devices in the late 2000s brought about another significant shift. Smartphones and tablets became ubiquitous, enabling access to educational content anytime and anywhere. This mobility transformed the learning experience, allowing students to engage with interactive apps and resources that complemented traditional learning materials. Educators began to explore the potential of gamification, harnessing game design elements to increase student engagement and motivation. The use of educational games and simulations created immersive experiences that made learning not just informative but also enjoyable.

The proliferation of social media further transformed educational practices, creating new avenues for collaboration and communication. Platforms like Twitter and Facebook fostered professional learning networks for educators, allowing them to share resources, strategies, and experiences. This connectivity encouraged a culture of continuous learning and professional development, enabling educators to stay current with emerging trends and best practices in teaching.

In recent years, the integration of data analytics into education has provided powerful insights into student learning patterns. By analyzing data collected from LMS platforms and educational apps, educators can identify trends and tailor their instruction to meet individual student needs. This personalized approach marks a significant evolution in educational technology, allowing for targeted interventions and support. It empowers educators to move away from a one-size-fits-all model, recognizing the unique strengths and challenges of each learner.

The challenges and opportunities presented by educational technology continue to evolve. While the benefits are clear, issues such as digital equity and access remain pressing concerns. Not all students have equal access to technology, which can exacerbate existing inequalities in education. As schools and educators navigate this landscape, it is crucial to prioritize inclusivity and ensure that all students have the resources they need to succeed.

The role of educators in this evolving landscape cannot be overstated. As technology becomes more prevalent in classrooms, teachers must adapt their practices to leverage these tools effectively. Professional development focused on technology integration is essential, providing educators with the skills and confidence to incorporate innovative resources into their teaching. Collaboration among educators, technologists, and policymakers is vital to create an environment where technology enhances, rather than hinders, the learning experience.

As we reflect on the history and evolution of educational technology, it is evident that each advancement has built upon the previous one, creating a dynamic and ever-changing landscape. From the humble beginnings of chalkboards and textbooks to the immersive experiences offered through virtual reality, the journey of EdTech is a testament to human ingenuity and the relentless pursuit of knowledge.

Moving forward, the future of educational technology holds immense promise. As emerging technologies like artificial intelligence and machine learning continue to develop, they will undoubtedly shape the next chapter of education. These tools have the potential to further personalize learning experiences, providing real-time feedback and adaptive pathways tailored to individual student needs.

However, with great power comes great responsibility. Educators, administrators, and policymakers must remain vigilant in addressing the ethical implications of technology in education. Issues such as data privacy, the digital divide, and the potential for bias in algorithms must be carefully considered to ensure that the advancements in EdTech serve all learners equitably.

The evolution of educational technology is not just about the tools themselves but also about the transformative impact they have on teaching and learning. As we embrace the future, it is essential to remember that at the heart of education is the relationship between teachers and students. Technology should enhance this connection, providing educators with innovative ways to engage, inspire, and empower their students.

In conclusion, the journey of educational technology is an ongoing story, one that reflects our collective aspirations for a more effective and inclusive education system. As we navigate this landscape, it is crucial to remain adaptable, open-minded, and committed to the idea that learning is a lifelong endeavor, enriched by the tools and technologies that continue to evolve. Embracing this change with a focus on improving educational outcomes for all learners will ensure that we keep moving forward, creating a brighter future for education.

Key Drivers of Digital Transformation in Education

Digital transformation in education is a multifaceted phenomenon that has reshaped the ways in which learning and teaching occur. Understanding the key drivers behind this transformation is essential for educators, administrators, and policymakers aiming to harness technology effectively to improve educational outcomes. Several factors contribute to this shift, each interlinked and influential in its own right.

One of the primary drivers is the rapid advancement of technology itself. The proliferation of high-speed internet, smartphones, tablets, and other digital devices has created an environment where information is more accessible than ever. Students today have grown up in a digital world, accustomed to receiving information instantaneously. This familiarity with technology encourages educational institutions to integrate digital tools into their curricula. Schools and universities are increasingly adopting Learning Management Systems (LMS) that allow for the seamless management of courses, assignments, and assessments. These platforms not only streamline administrative tasks but also enhance communication between educators and students, fostering a more collaborative learning environment.

Another significant factor is the demand for personalized learning experiences. Traditional one-size-fits-all approaches to education often fail to meet the diverse needs of learners. Digital tools enable educators to tailor their instruction to individual student preferences and learning styles. Data analytics play a crucial role here, allowing teachers to track student progress in real time and adjust their teaching methods accordingly. By leveraging data, educators can identify areas where students struggle and implement targeted interventions. This personalized approach not only boosts student engagement but also enhances overall learning outcomes.

Moreover, the global shift towards competency-based education is reshaping the educational landscape. As employers increasingly seek graduates with specific skills rather than mere degrees, educational institutions are adapting their curricula to focus on competencies. This shift necessitates the use of technology to assess student skills effectively. Digital assessments, simulations, and interactive learning environments facilitate the evaluation of competencies in a way that traditional exams cannot. By aligning educational programs with real-world skills, institutions better prepare students for the workforce, ensuring that they are not just knowledgeable but also capable.

The influence of the COVID-19 pandemic cannot be overlooked in discussions about digital transformation. The sudden shift to remote learning forced educators to adopt digital tools rapidly. This unprecedented situation highlighted both the potential and the challenges of technology in education. Many institutions were caught off guard, lacking the necessary infrastructure and training to transition smoothly. However, the experience also sparked innovation, as educators experimented with various online platforms and teaching methods. The lessons learned during this period have led to a greater acceptance of hybrid learning models, which combine in-person and digital instruction, thereby broadening educational access.

Equity and accessibility are also driving forces behind the digital transformation in education. As educational leaders recognize the disparities in access to technology and internet connectivity, there is a concerted effort to address these gaps. Initiatives aimed at providing devices and internet access to underserved communities are becoming increasingly common. The goal is to ensure that all students, regardless of their socioeconomic status, can benefit from digital learning resources. By prioritizing equity, educational institutions can create a more inclusive environment where every student has the opportunity to succeed.

The growing emphasis on lifelong learning further propels the transformation. In a rapidly changing job market, skills quickly become outdated. As a result, individuals are seeking continuous learning opportunities to remain competitive. Online courses, webinars, and micro-credential programs offer flexible options for professional development, appealing to both traditional students and working professionals. Educational institutions are responding by expanding their offerings to include non-degree programs that focus on specific skills or competencies. This shift not only meets the needs of learners but also positions institutions as key players in the lifelong learning ecosystem.

Collaboration among educational institutions, technology companies, and other stakeholders is essential for driving digital transformation. Partnerships can lead to the development of innovative solutions that address specific educational challenges. For instance, tech companies can provide the necessary tools and platforms, while educators can offer insights into effective teaching practices. Such collaborations can also facilitate the sharing of best practices and resources, leading to improved outcomes across the board. When all parties work together, the potential for transformative change in education increases significantly.

Furthermore, the role of student agency in the digital transformation cannot be understated. Today's learners are not passive recipients of information; they are active participants in their education. With access to a wealth of online resources, students can take charge of their learning journeys, exploring topics that interest them and collaborating with peers across the globe. This sense of agency fosters critical thinking and problem-solving skills, preparing students to navigate the complexities of the modern world. Educational institutions that empower students to take ownership of their learning are likely to see greater engagement and success.

The importance of professional development for educators is another crucial driver of digital transformation. As technology evolves, so too must the skills of teachers. Ongoing training programs focused on technology integration are essential to equip educators with the knowledge and confidence needed to use digital tools effectively. Professional development should not be a one-time event; instead, it should be an ongoing process that encourages collaboration and the sharing of experiences among educators. Institutions that prioritize the continuous growth of their teaching staff are better positioned to implement successful digital initiatives.

Lastly, the cultural shift within educational institutions plays a vital role in facilitating digital transformation. Embracing a culture of innovation encourages experimentation and risk-taking among educators. Institutions that are open to change are more likely to adopt new technologies and teaching methods. This cultural shift must be supported by leadership that values and promotes innovation, providing the resources and support necessary for educators to thrive. When a school or university fosters a culture of continuous improvement, it sets the stage for meaningful and lasting change.

Digital transformation in education is not merely about integrating technology; it is about rethinking the very essence of teaching and learning. The key drivers behind this transformation—technological advancements, personalized learning, competency-based education, the impact of recent global events, equity, lifelong learning, collaboration, student agency, professional development, and cultural shifts—work together to create a more dynamic and effective educational landscape. As educators and institutions embrace these drivers, they not only enhance the learning experience but also prepare students for a future that is increasingly shaped by technology and innovation. The journey of transformation is ongoing, and its success depends on the collective efforts of all stakeholders committed to fostering an educational environment that is responsive to the needs of learners today and tomorrow.

The Role of Technology in Modern Classrooms

The integration of technology in modern classrooms has revolutionized the educational landscape, transforming traditional teaching methods into dynamic, interactive experiences. As educators increasingly embrace digital tools, the role of technology extends beyond mere enhancement; it fundamentally reshapes how students learn, engage, and interact within their educational environments.

At the heart of this transformation is the shift from passive to active learning. In traditional classrooms, students often assumed a passive role, absorbing information from lectures and textbooks. However, with the introduction of technology, learners are now encouraged to participate actively in their education. Interactive whiteboards, tablets, and laptops allow students to engage with content in real time, fostering collaboration and encouraging discussions. For instance, using digital platforms like Google Classroom, teachers can facilitate group projects where students contribute ideas, conduct research, and present findings collectively. This approach not only promotes teamwork but also cultivates critical thinking skills as students navigate the complexities of working together.

Moreover, technology provides access to a wealth of resources that were previously out of reach. With the internet at their fingertips, students can explore vast libraries of information, educational videos, and interactive simulations. This abundance of resources enables personalized learning experiences tailored to individual interests and needs. For example, a student passionate about marine biology can dive into online courses, documentaries, and virtual field trips that supplement classroom learning, enhancing their understanding and engagement. This self-directed exploration empowers students to take ownership of their education, fostering a sense of agency that is crucial for lifelong learning.

The role of technology also extends to assessment and feedback. Traditional testing methods often fail to capture a student's full understanding or skills. In contrast, digital assessments can provide immediate feedback, helping educators identify areas where students struggle. Tools like formative assessment apps allow teachers to gauge understanding during lessons through quick polls or quizzes, enabling them to adjust their instruction on the spot. This real-time feedback loop not only supports student learning but also allows teachers to refine their teaching strategies, ensuring that they meet the needs of all learners.

Furthermore, technology enhances inclusivity in the classroom. Students with diverse learning needs can benefit from various digital tools designed to support different learning styles. For instance, text-to-speech software can assist students with reading difficulties, while interactive simulations can engage visual learners more effectively than traditional texts. By integrating technology, educators can create an environment that accommodates all students, fostering a sense of belonging and promoting equity in education.

The use of technology also prepares students for the demands of the modern workforce. As industries increasingly rely on digital tools and platforms, it is essential for students to develop digital literacy skills. Technology in the classroom provides opportunities for students to learn essential skills such as coding, data analysis, and digital communication. These competencies are not only valuable in academic settings but are also critical for success in a rapidly evolving job market. Schools that prioritize technology integration equip students with the skills they need to thrive in a world that is increasingly interconnected and technology-driven.

Moreover, technology facilitates communication and collaboration beyond the classroom walls. Virtual learning environments enable students to connect with peers and educators from around the globe. This exposure to diverse perspectives enhances cultural awareness and fosters global citizenship. For example, a classroom project that partners students with a school in another country can lead to rich exchanges of ideas and experiences, broadening students' horizons and promoting empathy. Such collaborations prepare students to navigate an increasingly globalized society, fostering skills that are essential for future success.

While the advantages of integrating technology in education are clear, challenges remain. One significant concern is the digital divide, which highlights disparities in access to technology and high-speed internet. Students from low-income families may struggle to keep up with their peers due to limited access to devices or reliable internet connections. Educators and policymakers must work collaboratively to address these inequities, ensuring that all students have the resources necessary to benefit from technology-enhanced learning.

Additionally, the role of educators is evolving in this technology-rich environment. As facilitators of learning, teachers must adapt their instructional practices to effectively integrate digital tools. Professional development focused on technology integration is essential to equip educators with the skills they need to utilize these tools effectively. Schools should foster a culture of continuous learning, encouraging educators to share best practices and collaborate on innovative teaching strategies. When teachers feel supported and empowered, they are more likely to embrace technology and leverage it to enhance student learning.

Another concern is the potential for technology to distract students rather than engage them. With the myriad of online distractions available, maintaining student focus can be challenging. Educators must strike a balance between leveraging technology for learning and minimizing distractions. Establishing clear guidelines for technology use in the classroom, coupled with explicit instruction on digital citizenship, can help students understand the importance of responsible technology use. Teaching students to navigate online distractions equips them with skills that are essential for their academic and personal lives.

The future of technology in the classroom is promising, as innovations continue to emerge. Virtual reality (VR) and augmented reality (AR) are beginning to play a significant role in education, offering immersive experiences that enhance learning. Imagine a history class where students can virtually walk through ancient civilizations or a science class where they can explore the human body in 3D. Such experiences deepen understanding and engagement, making learning more memorable and impactful.

In addition, artificial intelligence (AI) is poised to revolutionize personalized learning further. Adaptive learning technologies can analyze student performance data and adjust content delivery to suit individual needs. This level of customization holds the potential to further enhance student engagement and outcomes, ensuring that each learner receives the support they require to succeed.

As technology continues to evolve, the role of educators will remain crucial in guiding students through this digital landscape. Teachers must foster critical thinking, creativity, and collaboration, helping students navigate the complexities of modern life. By integrating technology thoughtfully and purposefully, educators can create learning environments that inspire curiosity, promote engagement, and prepare students for the challenges of the future.

In conclusion, technology plays a transformative role in modern classrooms, reshaping the ways students learn and interact. From fostering active learning and personalized experiences to enhancing inclusivity and preparing students for the workforce, the impact of technology is profound. While challenges exist, the potential for positive change is immense. By embracing technology as a tool for innovation and engagement, educators can create dynamic learning experiences that empower students to thrive in an increasingly digital world. The journey of integrating technology in education is ongoing, and the commitment to creating inclusive, engaging, and effective learning environments will continue to shape the future of education.

An Overview of Current EdTech Trends

The educational technology landscape is evolving rapidly, driven by innovations that reshape how learning occurs. As we navigate this dynamic environment, understanding the current trends is essential for educators, administrators, and students alike. These trends not only enhance the learning experience but also address the diverse needs of today's learners.

One prominent trend is the rise of blended learning models, which combine traditional face-to-face instruction with online learning. This approach allows educators to leverage the strengths of both methods, creating a more flexible and engaging learning environment. In a blended classroom, students can access course materials online, engage in interactive activities, and participate in discussions, all while benefiting from direct interaction with their teachers. This model has gained traction, particularly following the global shift to remote learning during the pandemic, which highlighted the advantages of digital resources.

Personalized learning is another significant trend reshaping education. As educators recognize that each student learns differently, they are increasingly adopting strategies that cater to individual learning styles and paces. Technology enables this personalization through adaptive learning platforms that provide tailored content based on student performance. For example, programs can assess a student's strengths and weaknesses, adjusting the difficulty of tasks accordingly. This approach not only fosters engagement but also ensures that students receive the support they need to succeed.

Gamification has emerged as a powerful tool to enhance student motivation and engagement. By incorporating game-like elements into educational activities, educators can create an interactive and enjoyable learning experience. Points, badges, and leaderboards are common features that encourage students to participate actively and strive for improvement. For instance, a history teacher might use a quiz game to review key concepts, making learning fun while reinforcing knowledge. This trend demonstrates that education does not have to be a monotonous process; instead, it can be an exciting journey.

The integration of artificial intelligence into educational tools is also gaining momentum. AI-driven platforms can analyze vast amounts of data to provide insights into student performance, enabling educators to make informed decisions about instruction. For example, AI can identify patterns in a student's learning behavior, helping teachers to tailor their approaches more effectively. Additionally, AI-powered chatbots can offer immediate support to students, answering questions and providing resources outside of classroom hours. This level of responsiveness enhances the learning experience and ensures that students feel supported.

Moreover, the use of immersive technologies, such as virtual reality (VR) and augmented reality (AR), is transforming how students engage with content. These technologies allow learners to experience concepts in a tangible way, creating memorable learning moments. Imagine a science class where students can virtually explore the human body or a history class that transports them to ancient civilizations. Such immersive experiences deepen understanding and spark curiosity, making complex subjects more accessible and engaging.

Another trend is the increasing emphasis on social and emotional learning (SEL) within educational settings. As educators recognize the importance of addressing students' emotional well-being, they are integrating SEL into their curricula. Technology plays a vital role in this trend by offering resources and tools that promote self-awareness, empathy, and relationship-building skills. Online platforms can provide students with scenarios to practice social skills or access mindfulness exercises that help them manage stress. By prioritizing SEL, educators create a more holistic approach to education that nurtures both academic and emotional growth.

The shift towards competency-based education is reshaping traditional grading systems. Rather than relying solely on standardized tests, many institutions are adopting models that focus on students demonstrating mastery of specific skills and knowledge. Digital portfolios allow students to showcase their work and progress, providing a more comprehensive view of their abilities. This trend emphasizes the importance of real-world skills, preparing students for future careers by equipping them with the competencies that employers value.

Collaboration and communication tools are becoming integral to modern classrooms. Platforms like Microsoft Teams and Slack facilitate collaboration among students, allowing them to work together on projects regardless of their physical location. This collaborative spirit extends beyond the classroom, enabling educators to connect with colleagues and share best practices. By fostering a culture of collaboration, technology helps break down silos and encourages a more inclusive and supportive educational environment.

Data-driven decision-making is another critical trend shaping educational practices. With access to extensive data on student performance, educators can make informed choices about curriculum design and instructional strategies. Learning analytics tools provide insights into how students engage with content, enabling teachers to identify trends and adjust their approaches accordingly. This data-informed approach not only enhances the learning experience but also ensures that resources are allocated effectively to support student success.

As technology continues to advance, the focus on accessibility and inclusivity in education is more important than ever. Educators are increasingly aware of the need to create environments where all students can thrive, regardless of their backgrounds or abilities. Digital tools that support diverse learning needs, such as screen readers and captioning services, are essential for ensuring that every student has equal access to educational resources. This trend reflects a broader commitment to equity in education, recognizing that technology can be a powerful equalizer when used thoughtfully.

The global shift toward remote and hybrid learning models has also influenced current trends in education. As institutions adapt to the realities of a post-pandemic world, many are embracing flexible learning options that accommodate diverse student needs. This shift requires a reevaluation of traditional teaching practices, with a focus on creating engaging and interactive online experiences. Educators are experimenting with synchronous and asynchronous learning formats, finding innovative ways to maintain student engagement and foster a sense of community, even in virtual environments.

Finally, the importance of digital citizenship is gaining recognition as students navigate an increasingly digital world. As technology becomes more integrated into daily life, it is essential for students to develop the skills needed to navigate online spaces responsibly. Educators are incorporating lessons on digital citizenship into their curricula, teaching students about online safety, privacy, and ethical behavior. This emphasis on responsible technology use equips students with the tools they need to thrive in a digital landscape, ensuring they are not only consumers of information but also responsible contributors to online communities.

As we reflect on these trends, it is clear that the landscape of educational technology is continually evolving. Each trend highlights the potential for technology to enhance the learning experience, making education more engaging, personalized, and accessible. Educators who stay informed about these developments are better equipped to create learning environments that prepare students for the challenges of tomorrow. Embracing these trends is not just about adopting new tools; it is about reimagining the educational experience to meet the diverse needs of today's learners. The future of education is bright, filled with opportunities for innovation and growth. By leveraging the power of technology, educators can inspire a new generation of learners to explore, create, and thrive in an ever-changing world.

Challenges and Opportunities in EdTech Adoption

The landscape of educational technology is rich with potential, yet it is not without its challenges. As schools and institutions strive to adopt new technologies, they must navigate a complex array of obstacles while recognizing the unique opportunities that these innovations present. Understanding both the challenges and opportunities in EdTech adoption is crucial for educators and administrators aiming to enhance the learning experience.

One of the most pressing challenges is the digital divide. Access to technology is not uniform; many students from low-income families lack the necessary devices or reliable internet connections. This disparity creates significant barriers to equitable learning opportunities. While some students thrive in technology-rich environments, others are left behind, unable to participate fully in digital learning experiences. Schools must prioritize initiatives that bridge this gap, ensuring that all students have access to the resources they need. This might include partnerships with community organizations to provide devices, or initiatives that expand internet access in underserved areas.

Professional development is another critical aspect of successful EdTech adoption. Many educators feel unprepared to integrate technology effectively into their teaching practices. Without adequate training, teachers may struggle to utilize new tools to their fullest potential, leading to frustration and underwhelming results. Institutions should invest in ongoing professional development that equips educators with the skills and confidence to navigate the ever-evolving landscape of educational technology. This training should not only focus on technical skills but also on pedagogical strategies that enhance learning through technology.

Resistance to change can significantly impede the adoption of new technologies. Many educators and administrators may be hesitant to abandon traditional teaching methods in favor of digital tools. This reluctance often stems from comfort with familiar practices or a lack of understanding of the benefits that technology can bring. To address this resistance, stakeholders must foster a culture of innovation within educational institutions. This involves showcasing successful case studies, providing opportunities for peer collaboration, and creating an environment where experimentation with new tools is encouraged. When educators see the positive impact of technology on student engagement and learning outcomes, they are more likely to embrace change.

Another challenge lies in the integration of technology into existing curricula. Simply introducing new tools is not enough; they must be thoughtfully aligned with learning objectives. Educators often struggle to find the right balance between traditional content and digital resources. To overcome this hurdle, institutions should promote collaborative planning among educators. By working together to design lessons that incorporate technology meaningfully, teachers can ensure that digital tools enhance rather than detract from the learning experience.

Data privacy and security present additional concerns in the realm of EdTech. With the increasing use of digital platforms, schools must be vigilant in protecting student data. Parents and educators alike are right to be concerned about how personal information is collected, stored, and used. Institutions must establish clear policies and practices regarding data privacy, ensuring compliance with regulations and fostering trust among stakeholders. By prioritizing transparency and security, schools can create a safe environment for digital learning.

Despite these challenges, the opportunities presented by EdTech adoption are significant. Enhanced engagement is one of the most compelling benefits. Technology has the power to transform passive learning into interactive experiences that capture students' attention. Tools like gamified learning platforms and interactive simulations can make complex subjects more accessible and enjoyable. For example, a science lesson that incorporates virtual lab experiments allows students to explore concepts hands-on, deepening their understanding and sparking curiosity.

Personalized learning is another area where technology shines. Digital tools can facilitate tailored learning experiences that meet individual student needs. Adaptive learning platforms assess student performance in real time, adjusting content and delivery to suit each learner. This personalized approach not only increases engagement but also promotes mastery of content. Educators can use data analytics to identify areas where students struggle, enabling targeted interventions that enhance learning outcomes.

Collaboration and communication are also enhanced through technology. Digital platforms facilitate collaboration among students, enabling them to work together on projects regardless of physical location. Tools like shared documents and discussion forums foster teamwork and peer interaction. This collaborative spirit extends to educators, who can connect with colleagues globally to share resources and best practices. By leveraging technology to build communities of practice, educators can enhance their professional growth and improve classroom outcomes.

The potential for scalability in educational technology is significant. Digital resources can be easily replicated and shared, allowing successful practices to reach a broader audience. Online courses, webinars, and instructional videos can provide valuable professional development opportunities for educators, irrespective of their geographical location. This scalability enables institutions to respond quickly to emerging trends and challenges, adapting their practices to meet the evolving needs of students.

Furthermore, the ability to gather and analyze data is a powerful opportunity in EdTech adoption. Data-driven decision-making allows educators to monitor student progress, identify trends, and refine instructional practices. With access to real-time analytics, educators can make informed choices that enhance the learning experience. This emphasis on data not only supports individualized learning but also fosters a culture of continuous improvement within educational institutions.

The COVID-19 pandemic has accelerated the adoption of technology in education, highlighting both challenges and opportunities. As schools transitioned to remote learning, many educators discovered innovative ways to engage students, often exceeding their initial expectations. The necessity of digital learning fostered creativity and adaptability among educators, leading to the development of new instructional strategies that can continue to benefit students in hybrid or in-person settings. This shift has prompted a reevaluation of what effective teaching looks like in the 21st century.

Embracing a growth mindset is essential for overcoming the challenges of EdTech adoption. Educators and administrators must view technology as a tool for enhancement rather than a replacement for traditional methods. By fostering a culture of experimentation, schools can encourage educators to explore new tools and approaches. Celebrating successes and learning from failures will create an environment where innovation thrives, ultimately benefiting students.

In conclusion, the journey of adopting educational technology is fraught with challenges but also rich with opportunities. Addressing the digital divide, investing in professional development, overcoming resistance to change, ensuring data privacy, and integrating technology thoughtfully into curricula are all essential steps for successful implementation. At the same time, the potential for enhanced engagement, personalized learning, collaboration, scalability, and data-driven decision-making presents exciting possibilities for educators and students alike. By navigating these challenges with a proactive and innovative mindset, educational institutions can harness the full power of technology to transform learning for all students. The future of education is bright, filled with opportunities to create more equitable, engaging, and effective learning environments.

Chapter 2: Digital Learning Platforms and Tools

Learning Management Systems (LMS): Overview and Applications

Learning Management Systems (LMS) have become essential tools in the realm of education, revolutionizing how educators deliver content and how students engage with learning materials. These platforms serve as centralized hubs where teachers can manage courses, track student progress, and facilitate communication. Understanding the breadth of LMS applications and their benefits is crucial for educators seeking to enhance their teaching practices and improve student outcomes.

At their core, LMS platforms provide a structured environment for delivering educational content. They allow educators to create and organize course materials, including lectures, readings, assignments, and assessments. By consolidating these resources in one place, LMS platforms streamline the learning process, making it easier for students to navigate their courses. This centralization is particularly beneficial in hybrid or fully online learning environments, where students may otherwise struggle to find and access materials.

One of the most significant advantages of using an LMS is the ability to facilitate asynchronous learning. Students can access course materials at their convenience, allowing them to learn at their own pace. This flexibility is particularly valuable for diverse learners who may require additional time to grasp complex concepts. For instance, a student juggling work and family responsibilities can engage with course content during their available hours, improving their chances of success. This adaptability also extends to various learning styles, as students can revisit materials, such as recorded lectures or interactive modules, as often as needed.

Assessment capabilities within LMS platforms provide a robust framework for tracking student progress. Educators can create quizzes, tests, and assignments that automatically grade and provide immediate feedback. This feature not only saves time for instructors but also allows students to understand their strengths and weaknesses in real time. For example, a math teacher might assign a quiz on algebra concepts that provides instant feedback, helping students identify areas for improvement before moving on to more advanced topics. This immediate feedback loop fosters a growth mindset, encouraging students to take ownership of their learning journey.

Analytics tools integrated within LMS platforms further enhance their utility. Educators can generate reports on student engagement, participation rates, and assessment scores, enabling them to make data-driven decisions. By analyzing trends, teachers can identify patterns, such as which topics students find most challenging or whether specific instructional strategies are effective. This insight allows for timely interventions, ensuring that no student falls behind. For instance, if data reveals that many students struggled with a particular module, the educator can modify the approach, perhaps by offering additional resources or targeted support.

Collaboration features within LMS platforms foster a sense of community among students, even in online or hybrid settings. Discussion boards, group projects, and peer review tools encourage interaction, allowing students to learn from one another. This collaborative environment mimics real-world scenarios, where teamwork and communication are paramount. For example, in a literature course, students can engage in discussions about readings, sharing insights and interpretations that deepen their understanding of the material. Such interactions not only enhance learning but also help develop critical soft skills essential for future careers.

The integration of multimedia elements into LMS platforms enriches the learning experience. Educators can incorporate videos, podcasts, and interactive simulations, appealing to various learning preferences. For instance, a science teacher might use a virtual lab simulation to demonstrate chemical reactions, providing students with a hands-on experience without the constraints of a physical lab. This multimedia approach not only captures students' attention but also deepens their understanding by catering to different learning modalities.

Another vital aspect of LMS platforms is their role in facilitating ongoing communication between educators and students. Announcements, messaging features, and feedback tools enable timely communication, ensuring that students remain informed and engaged. This open line of communication is particularly crucial in online learning environments, where students may feel isolated. By fostering a supportive atmosphere, educators can help students feel connected, ultimately enhancing their motivation and commitment to their studies.

Despite the numerous advantages of LMS platforms, challenges do exist. One common concern is the initial learning curve associated with adopting new technology. Educators may feel overwhelmed by the multitude of features and options available. To address this, institutions should provide comprehensive training and support. Professional development sessions, resource guides, and peer mentorship can facilitate a smoother transition to using an LMS effectively. When educators feel confident in their ability to navigate the platform, they are more likely to utilize its full potential.

Another challenge is ensuring that all students have equitable access to the necessary technology. While LMS platforms enhance learning opportunities, they can also exacerbate existing disparities if students lack reliable internet access or devices. Schools must prioritize initiatives that address these gaps, such as providing technology loans or establishing community Wi-Fi hotspots. By ensuring that every student has the tools they need to succeed, institutions can create a more equitable learning environment.

Data privacy and security also merit consideration when implementing LMS platforms. Educators and institutions must protect student information and ensure compliance with relevant regulations. Clear policies regarding data use and privacy should be communicated to all stakeholders. Additionally, selecting LMS providers that prioritize security measures can help mitigate risks and foster trust among students and parents.

As technology continues to evolve, so too do the capabilities of LMS platforms. Innovations such as artificial intelligence and machine learning are beginning to shape the future of these systems. For example, personalized learning experiences powered by AI can adapt content delivery based on individual student performance, further enhancing engagement and outcomes. The potential to integrate virtual reality experiences into LMS platforms also opens new avenues for immersive learning, allowing students to explore complex subjects in ways previously unimaginable.

To maximize the benefits of an LMS, educators should consider implementing best practices for course design and delivery. Clear learning objectives should guide the development of course materials, ensuring alignment between assessments and instructional strategies. Regularly updating content and incorporating student feedback can enhance the relevance and effectiveness of the course. Engaging students in the course design process fosters a sense of ownership, making them more invested in their learning.

Establishing a supportive community of practice among educators can also enhance the effectiveness of LMS adoption. By sharing experiences, strategies, and resources, educators can learn from one another and continuously improve their practices. Collaborative planning sessions, where educators work together to design integrated lessons, can lead to innovative approaches that benefit all students.

In conclusion, Learning Management Systems are powerful tools that can significantly enhance the educational experience. By providing a centralized platform for course management, assessment, collaboration, and communication, LMS platforms empower educators to create engaging and effective learning environments. While challenges such as the digital divide, training needs, and data privacy must be addressed, the opportunities for personalized learning, enhanced engagement, and data-driven decision-making are immense. As educators embrace these systems and continually adapt their practices, they can transform their classrooms into dynamic spaces where all students have the opportunity to thrive. The future of education is bright, with LMS platforms playing a pivotal role in shaping the next generation of learners.

The Rise of Massive Open Online Courses (MOOCs)

The emergence of Massive Open Online Courses (MOOCs) has transformed the landscape of education, making high-quality learning experiences accessible to a global audience. These online courses, often offered by prestigious institutions, have democratized education in ways that were previously unimaginable. With the ability to enroll thousands of students at once, MOOCs break down geographical, financial, and institutional barriers, allowing learners from all walks of life to engage with content that might otherwise be out of reach.

The rise of MOOCs can be traced back to the early 2010s, when platforms like Coursera, edX, and Udacity began partnering with universities to offer free or low-cost courses. This model was revolutionary, as it leveraged technology to deliver content that was traditionally confined to the classroom. Students could now learn at their own pace, accessing lectures, readings, and discussion forums from anywhere with an internet connection. The appeal of MOOCs lies in their flexibility; learners can tailor their educational experiences to fit their schedules, making it easier for busy professionals, parents, and students to pursue their interests.

One of the most significant benefits of MOOCs is the variety of subjects available. Unlike traditional degree programs that may focus on a narrow curriculum, MOOCs cover an extensive range of topics, from computer science and data analysis to philosophy and art history. This diversity allows learners to explore new fields, develop new skills, or deepen their existing knowledge without the commitment of enrolling in a full degree program. For instance, someone working in marketing might choose to take a MOOC in data science to enhance their analytical capabilities, making them more valuable in their current role.

The interactive nature of MOOCs also contributes to their appeal. Many courses incorporate multimedia elements such as videos, quizzes, and discussion forums, making learning more engaging. Instructors often use real-world examples and case studies, allowing students to apply theoretical concepts to practical situations. This active learning approach not only enhances understanding but also encourages critical thinking and problem-solving skills. Moreover, the opportunity to interact with a diverse cohort of learners fosters a sense of community, even in a virtual environment. Students can share insights, ask questions, and collaborate on projects, enriching their educational experience.

Assessment in MOOCs varies from traditional educational settings, often utilizing peer-reviewed assignments and automated quizzes. This innovative approach allows for continuous feedback, giving students a chance to reflect on their learning and improve. For example, in a course on creative writing, participants might submit their work for peer review, receiving constructive feedback from fellow students. This collaborative assessment process not only builds a sense of community but also encourages learners to engage critically with the material.

Despite their many advantages, MOOCs also face challenges that can impact their effectiveness. One significant concern is the high dropout rate associated with these courses. While many students enroll with enthusiasm, a substantial number do not complete the courses. Factors contributing to this phenomenon include the lack of accountability in self-paced learning environments, the overwhelming volume of content, and the difficulty of maintaining motivation without face-to-face interaction. To address these issues, course designers are exploring strategies to enhance learner engagement and support, such as incorporating regular check-ins, providing personalized feedback, and fostering online communities.

Another challenge is the perception of MOOCs in the job market. While many employers recognize the value of skills gained through MOOCs, some still regard them with skepticism, viewing them as inferior to traditional degrees. This perception can deter potential learners from pursuing MOOCs, particularly those seeking to enhance their career prospects. To counter this stigma, it is essential for MOOC providers to emphasize the quality of courses and the credentials offered. Many platforms now offer verified certificates or digital badges that learners can showcase on their resumes or LinkedIn profiles, signaling their commitment to professional development.

Moreover, the issue of quality control in MOOCs is paramount. With numerous courses available, not all are created equal. Some may lack rigorous content or competent instruction, leading to a poor learning experience. To ensure quality, MOOC platforms must implement robust evaluation processes, seeking feedback from participants and continually refining their offerings. Collaborations with respected universities and industry experts can help maintain high standards, ensuring that learners receive valuable, relevant education.

The role of technology in the success of MOOCs cannot be overstated. As internet access becomes more widespread and technology continues to evolve, the potential for MOOCs to reach even broader audiences increases. Mobile learning, for instance, is gaining traction, allowing students to access course materials on smartphones and tablets. This flexibility caters to learners who may not have access to a computer or prefer to learn on the go.

The future of MOOCs also lies in their ability to adapt to the changing landscape of education. As educational needs evolve, so too must the content and delivery methods of MOOCs. Trends such as micro-credentialing and competency-based education are gaining popularity, offering learners the chance to earn specific skills or credentials rather than completing an entire course. This shift aligns with the needs of today's job market, where employers increasingly seek candidates with targeted skills rather than traditional degrees.

In addition to individual learners, organizations are beginning to recognize the value of MOOCs for employee training and development. Companies can leverage these platforms to provide ongoing education for their staff, ensuring that employees remain competitive in an ever-changing business environment. This approach not only enhances workforce skills but also fosters a culture of continuous learning within organizations.

The impact of MOOCs on traditional education models is profound. As more learners turn to online education, traditional institutions are reevaluating their offerings. Many universities are beginning to incorporate online elements into their programs, recognizing the need for flexibility and accessibility. Hybrid models that combine in-person instruction with online components are becoming increasingly popular, allowing institutions to cater to diverse student needs.

The social impact of MOOCs is equally significant. By providing access to quality education, MOOCs can empower individuals from underrepresented communities, helping to bridge educational gaps. For instance, learners in remote areas may gain access to courses from prestigious universities that would otherwise be unavailable to them. This accessibility can lead to improved economic opportunities and foster a more informed society.

As MOOCs continue to evolve, it is essential for educators, learners, and policymakers to engage in ongoing dialogue about their role in the educational landscape. Collaborative efforts can help shape the future of online education, ensuring that it remains responsive to the needs of learners and society at large. By embracing the potential of MOOCs, we can transform education into a more inclusive, flexible, and dynamic experience.

In summary, the rise of Massive Open Online Courses has ushered in a new era of education, characterized by accessibility, flexibility, and interactivity. While challenges such as high dropout rates and perceptions of value persist, the opportunities for learning and growth are immense. As technology continues to advance and the demand for lifelong learning increases, MOOCs will play a crucial role in shaping the future of education. By harnessing their potential, we can create a more equitable and informed world, where education is truly within reach for everyone.

Interactive and Adaptive Learning Tools

The educational landscape has been profoundly transformed by the advent of interactive and adaptive learning tools, which have redefined how students engage with content and how educators deliver instruction. These tools not only enhance the learning experience but also cater to the diverse needs of learners, ensuring that education is more personalized and effective than ever before. Understanding the significance of these tools and how to implement them can empower educators to create dynamic learning environments that foster deeper understanding and engagement.

Interactive learning tools encompass a variety of technologies and methodologies designed to actively involve students in the learning process. Unlike traditional lecture-based approaches, these tools encourage participation and engagement through hands-on activities, simulations, and collaborative projects. For instance, platforms such as Kahoot! and Quizizz enable educators to create engaging quizzes and games that turn assessments into interactive experiences. This gamified approach not only boosts student engagement but also helps reinforce key concepts in a fun and memorable way.

Consider a classroom scenario where a teacher introduces a complex topic, such as the principles of physics. Rather than relying solely on textbook explanations, the educator can use simulations that allow students to visualize and manipulate variables. Tools like PhET Interactive Simulations provide a virtual environment where learners can experiment with different conditions, observing the outcomes of their actions in real time. This hands-on approach not only solidifies understanding but also cultivates critical thinking skills as students analyze their results and make connections to theoretical concepts.

Adaptive learning tools take personalization a step further by tailoring educational experiences to individual student needs. These platforms utilize data to assess a learner's strengths and weaknesses, adjusting the content and pace accordingly. For example, systems like DreamBox Learning and Smart Sparrow adapt in real time, providing customized exercises based on student performance. If a student struggles with a particular math concept, the tool can present additional practice problems or alternative explanations to help clarify the topic. This level of personalization ensures that each learner progresses at their own pace, reducing frustration and enhancing confidence.

Implementing interactive and adaptive tools requires a thoughtful approach. Educators should begin by identifying specific learning objectives and determining which tools align best with those goals. It's essential to consider the subject matter and the varying levels of student readiness. For instance, in a language arts class, interactive reading platforms like Newsela can provide articles at different reading levels, allowing students to engage with the same content while receiving appropriate support.

Professional development is also crucial for successful integration. Educators must feel comfortable using these tools and understanding their functionalities. Schools can offer training sessions, workshops, or peer mentoring programs to build confidence and competence among teachers. When educators are well-equipped, they can model the use of these tools effectively, guiding students through the learning process.

One of the remarkable aspects of interactive and adaptive learning tools is their ability to provide immediate feedback. In traditional educational settings, students often wait until assignments are graded to understand their performance. However, with adaptive tools, feedback is instantaneous. This immediacy allows students to reflect on their learning in real time, making adjustments as necessary. For example, in an adaptive math platform, a student who answers a question incorrectly receives immediate hints or explanations, enabling them to understand their mistakes and learn from them right away.

Another significant advantage of these tools is their capacity to promote collaboration among students. Interactive platforms often include features that allow learners to work together on projects, share insights, and provide peer feedback. This collaborative approach not only enhances learning but also fosters essential social skills. For instance, tools like Padlet or Google Jamboard enable students to contribute to a shared digital space, where they can brainstorm ideas, organize information, and collaborate on assignments. These interactions enrich the learning experience, as students learn from each other and develop a sense of community.

As educators implement these tools, it's important to monitor their effectiveness continuously. Collecting data on student performance and engagement can provide valuable insights into which tools are working and which may need adjustment. Many adaptive learning platforms offer built-in analytics that allow educators to track progress over time, helping them identify trends and make informed decisions about instruction. For example, if a particular group of students consistently struggles with a specific type of question, educators can adjust their teaching strategies or provide targeted interventions.

While interactive and adaptive learning tools offer numerous benefits, challenges do exist. One concern is the potential for over-reliance on technology. While these tools can enhance learning, they should not replace the essential human element of teaching. Educators must strike a balance between utilizing technology and fostering meaningful relationships with their students. Building rapport, understanding individual needs, and providing emotional support are aspects of teaching that technology cannot replicate.

Another challenge is ensuring equitable access to technology. Not all students have the same access to devices or reliable internet connections, which can create disparities in learning opportunities. Schools must take proactive steps to address these inequities by providing resources and support to all students. This might include lending devices, establishing community Wi-Fi hubs, or offering flexible learning options that accommodate various needs.

Moreover, the rapid pace of technological change poses its own set of challenges. Educators must stay informed about new tools and methodologies, which can be overwhelming. Professional development and collaborative learning communities can help educators navigate this landscape, sharing experiences and best practices to enhance their skills and knowledge.

As the landscape of education continues to evolve, interactive and adaptive learning tools will play an increasingly important role. Their ability to engage students actively, personalize learning experiences, and provide real-time feedback aligns with the needs of today's diverse learners. By embracing these tools, educators can create more dynamic and inclusive classrooms that foster deeper understanding and inspire lifelong learning.

Looking ahead, the future of education will likely see an even greater integration of these technologies. Innovations such as artificial intelligence and machine learning will enhance adaptive learning capabilities, allowing for even more personalized and responsive educational experiences. Virtual and augmented reality tools may also emerge, providing immersive learning environments that further engage students and enhance their understanding of complex concepts.

Ultimately, the success of interactive and adaptive learning tools hinges on the commitment of educators to thoughtfully integrate them into their teaching practices. By focusing on student-centered approaches and fostering a culture of collaboration and innovation, educators can harness the power of these tools to transform learning. The journey toward a more interactive and adaptive educational landscape is not just about technology; it's about creating meaningful experiences that empower students to thrive in an ever-changing world. Through intentional implementation, ongoing reflection, and a commitment to equity, the potential of interactive and adaptive learning tools can be fully realized, paving the way for a brighter future in education.

Gamification in Education: Engaging Students

Gamification in education has emerged as a powerful strategy to enhance student engagement and motivation. By integrating game-like elements into the learning process, educators can create immersive environments that stimulate interest and foster a love for learning. This approach transforms traditional educational experiences, making them interactive and enjoyable, ultimately leading to improved academic outcomes.

At its core, gamification involves applying game design principles to non-game contexts. In the classroom, this can manifest in various ways, such as point systems, badges, leaderboards, challenges, and narrative-driven quests. These elements tap into intrinsic motivations, encouraging students to participate actively and persist through challenges. For instance, consider a classroom where students earn points for completing assignments, participating in discussions, and helping peers. This system not only incentivizes academic engagement but also fosters a sense of community and collaboration among students.

One compelling aspect of gamification is its ability to create a sense of achievement. When students receive badges or rewards for reaching milestones, it reinforces their progress and encourages them to strive for further success. This recognition can be particularly impactful for learners who may struggle with traditional assessments. By celebrating small victories, educators can help build confidence and resilience. For example, a science teacher might award badges for mastering specific concepts, prompting students to take ownership of their learning journey.

The design of gamified experiences should align with learning objectives to ensure that educational content remains the primary focus. It's essential to strike a balance between fun and educational value. A well-designed gamified lesson not only engages students but also reinforces key concepts. For instance, a history teacher might create a quest where students role-play as historical figures, navigating challenges based on real events. This not only brings history to life but also deepens students' understanding of the subject matter.

Collaboration is another vital component of gamification. Many game-based learning platforms encourage teamwork, allowing students to work together to solve problems or complete challenges. This collaboration fosters communication skills and helps students learn from one another. For example, platforms like Classcraft enable students to form teams and tackle quests together, promoting a cooperative learning environment. In this way, gamification not only enhances individual learning but also cultivates essential social skills.

Incorporating storytelling elements into gamification can further enrich the educational experience. Narrative-driven learning engages students' imaginations and helps them connect emotionally with the material. When students encounter challenges within a story framework, they are more likely to invest themselves in finding solutions. For instance, a literature teacher might create a storyline where students must solve mysteries related to the characters in a novel. This approach encourages deeper analysis and critical thinking, as students are motivated to engage with the text to unravel the plot.

To implement gamification effectively, educators should start with clear learning objectives. Identifying what students should achieve through the gamified experience will guide the design process. For example, if the goal is to improve vocabulary skills, the educator might create a word-based game where students earn points for using new words in context. This clarity ensures that the gamification elements serve a purpose and enhance learning outcomes.

Feedback is a crucial aspect of the gamification process. Regular, constructive feedback helps students understand their progress and areas for improvement. In traditional educational settings, feedback can often be delayed, leading to missed opportunities for growth. Gamification allows for immediate feedback through quizzes, challenges, and peer assessments. For instance, if students engage in a game-based math platform that provides instant feedback, they can quickly adjust their strategies and improve their understanding of concepts.

While the benefits of gamification are evident, challenges may arise during implementation. One common concern is the risk of students focusing solely on rewards rather than the learning process. To mitigate this, educators should emphasize the intrinsic value of learning alongside extrinsic rewards. By fostering a growth mindset and helping students understand that the journey is just as important as the destination, educators can create a more balanced approach to gamification.

Additionally, not all students may respond positively to gamified experiences. Some may feel overwhelmed by competition or may not be motivated by rewards. It's essential for educators to differentiate instruction and provide various pathways for engagement. Offering choices in how students can earn points or recognition can help cater to diverse motivations. For example, while some students may thrive in competitive environments, others may prefer collaborative projects or creative assignments.

Technology can play a significant role in facilitating gamification. Numerous platforms and tools are available to help educators design engaging gamified experiences. For instance, platforms like Kahoot! and Nearpod allow teachers to create interactive quizzes and activities that capture students' attention. These tools often include features that enable real-time participation, making learning feel dynamic and engaging.

Moreover, the integration of gamification into online and blended learning environments has gained traction. With the rise of remote learning, educators have adapted gamified strategies to keep students engaged. Virtual escape rooms, online scavenger hunts, and interactive simulations are just a few examples of how gamification can thrive in digital spaces. These approaches not only maintain student interest but also help develop digital literacy skills essential for the modern world.

As educators explore gamification, it's crucial to assess its effectiveness continuously. Gathering data on student engagement, performance, and feedback can provide valuable insights into what works and what needs adjustment. Surveys, reflection journals, and informal check-ins can help educators gauge student perceptions and experiences with gamified elements. This iterative approach ensures that gamification remains relevant and beneficial for all learners.

The potential for gamification extends beyond the classroom. Schools can foster a culture of gamified learning by involving the entire school community, including parents and guardians. Encouraging family participation in gamified initiatives, such as challenges or competitions, can strengthen the connection between home and school. This collaborative effort reinforces the idea that learning is a shared journey and encourages a supportive learning environment.

Looking ahead, the future of gamification in education is promising. As technology continues to advance, new opportunities will arise for innovative gamified experiences. Virtual reality and augmented reality are poised to revolutionize how students interact with content, offering immersive experiences that deepen understanding. Imagine a biology class where students can explore the human body in 3D or a geography course where they can virtually travel to different countries. These experiences can further enhance engagement and make learning more relevant and impactful.

In conclusion, gamification in education represents a transformative approach to engaging students and enhancing learning. By integrating game-like elements, educators can create interactive, motivating environments that foster collaboration and creativity. While challenges exist, the benefits of increased engagement, personalized learning, and immediate feedback are significant. As educators thoughtfully implement gamified strategies and continually assess their effectiveness, they can foster a culture of enthusiasm for learning that prepares students for success in an ever-evolving world. By harnessing the power of gamification, educators can inspire a generation of learners who are not only knowledgeable but also passionate about their education.

Virtual and Augmented Reality in Learning Environments

The fusion of virtual and augmented reality into learning environments heralds a new era of educational possibilities. VR and AR technologies are not just about adding another layer to existing educational methods; they transform the very fabric of learning, offering immersive experiences that were previously unimaginable. By stepping into a digital realm, learners engage with content in ways that transcend traditional textbooks and lectures, making learning both interactive and impactful.

Picture a classroom where history comes to life. Through VR, students can walk the bustling streets of ancient Rome, hearing the ambient sounds of a thriving empire and engaging with historical figures. This immersive experience fosters a profound connection with the subject matter, allowing students to grasp complex historical events through firsthand interaction. Such experiences cultivate curiosity and inspire deeper investigations into the past, nurturing a genuine passion for learning.

Augmented Reality offers another dimension, blending digital information with the physical world. In a biology class, students can observe a 3D model of the human heart hovering above their desks, rotating it to explore its intricate anatomy. With real-time data overlays, AR provides context-sensitive information, enhancing comprehension and retention. The tactile, visual nature of AR caters to diverse learning styles, ensuring that complex subjects become accessible to all learners.

The integration of VR and AR in learning environments also encourages collaboration and creativity. In virtual spaces, students from different corners of the globe can convene, breaking down geographical barriers. They can work on projects together, simulate experiments, or engage in problem-solving activities. This fosters a sense of global citizenship and equips students with the skills needed to thrive in an interconnected world.

Moreover, these technologies cater to personalized learning experiences. With VR and AR, educators can tailor content to individual learning paces and preferences. Imagine a student struggling with geometry; through VR, they can manipulate and explore geometric shapes in a 3D space, gaining a tangible understanding of abstract concepts. This personalized approach not only boosts confidence but also enhances academic outcomes.

Educators play a pivotal role in this digital transformation. They become facilitators, guiding students through immersive experiences and helping them draw meaningful connections. Teachers can design VR and AR activities that align with curricular goals, ensuring that these technologies are not mere novelties but integral components of the learning process. Professional development and training are crucial in equipping educators with the skills to harness the full potential of VR and AR.

However, the adoption of these technologies comes with its challenges. Cost and accessibility remain significant barriers, with VR headsets and AR devices often requiring substantial investment. Schools and institutions must weigh the benefits against the financial implications, seeking partnerships and funding opportunities to bridge the gap. Additionally, there are concerns about screen time and the potential for digital fatigue. Balancing virtual experiences with offline activities is essential to ensure holistic development.

Ethical considerations also come into play, especially concerning data privacy and security. As students interact within virtual environments, their data may be collected and analyzed. Safeguarding this information is paramount, requiring robust policies and practices to protect users' privacy. Transparency and informed consent are vital components of a responsible VR and AR implementation strategy.

Despite these challenges, the potential of VR and AR in learning environments is immense. These technologies can democratize education, offering access to high-quality resources in regions where traditional educational infrastructure is lacking. Through mobile AR applications, students in remote areas can access interactive content, bridging educational divides and fostering inclusivity.

Furthermore, VR and AR prepare students for the future workplace, which increasingly values digital literacy and technological proficiency. By engaging with these technologies from an early age, students develop skills that are highly sought after in the modern job market. They learn to navigate virtual spaces, collaborate with digital tools, and think critically about technology's role in society.

The psychological benefits of VR and AR in education are equally compelling. Immersive learning can enhance motivation and engagement, reducing anxiety and improving overall well-being. By offering a safe space to explore and experiment, VR and AR empower students to take risks and learn from their mistakes, fostering resilience and adaptability.

Incorporating VR and AR into learning environments also stimulates innovation within the educational sector. Developers and educators collaborate to create novel applications and tools, pushing the boundaries of what is possible. This synergy fuels a continuous cycle of improvement and adaptation, ensuring that educational practices evolve alongside technological advancements.

As we stand on the brink of this educational revolution, it is crucial to approach VR and AR with a balanced perspective. While these technologies hold transformative potential, they must complement, rather than replace, traditional teaching methods. Striking this balance ensures that students receive a comprehensive education that prepares them for the complexities of the modern world.

In conclusion, virtual and augmented reality are not just tools; they are catalysts for change within learning environments. By embracing these technologies, we can create dynamic, engaging, and inclusive educational experiences that inspire lifelong learning. As educators, students, and technologists collaborate to shape the future of education, the possibilities are limitless.

Chapter 3: Personalizing Education Through Technology

Data-Driven Personalization in Education

Imagine a classroom where each student's learning journey is uniquely tailored to their needs, strengths, and interests. Data-driven personalization in education is not just a futuristic concept; it's a transformative approach that's reshaping how educators deliver content and how students engage with their studies. This innovative method leverages data analytics to create a more individualized and effective learning experience for every student.

At the heart of data-driven personalization lies the ability to collect and analyze vast amounts of information. This data can come from various sources, including student assessments, participation in class activities, homework performance, and even engagement on digital platforms. By processing this data, educators can gain invaluable insights into each student's learning patterns, preferences, and challenges. These insights empower teachers to make informed decisions about instructional strategies and tailor them to meet the specific needs of their students.

Consider a student struggling with algebra. Traditional teaching methods might not address the underlying issues causing their difficulties. However, through data analysis, a teacher might identify that the student excels in visual learning but struggles with abstract concepts. Armed with this knowledge, the teacher can introduce visual aids, interactive simulations, and real-world applications to help the student grasp algebraic principles more effectively. This targeted approach not only boosts the student's understanding but also enhances their confidence and motivation.

The benefits of data-driven personalization extend beyond academic achievements. By fostering a more engaging and relevant learning environment, this approach nurtures a love for learning and encourages students to take ownership of their educational journey. When students see that their unique needs are being considered, they become more invested in their studies, leading to a deeper commitment to their educational goals.

Data-driven personalization also plays a crucial role in identifying and supporting students with diverse learning needs. For instance, students with learning disabilities often require specialized interventions that traditional teaching methods might not provide. Through data analysis, educators can detect patterns that indicate these needs early on, allowing them to implement targeted interventions and accommodations. This proactive approach ensures that all students receive the support they need to thrive academically and personally.

Moreover, data-driven personalization helps bridge the gap between home and school. By sharing data insights with parents and guardians, educators can foster a collaborative partnership that supports the student's learning journey. Parents gain a better understanding of their child's strengths and challenges, enabling them to provide meaningful support and encouragement at home. This collaboration empowers students to excel in their studies and develop a sense of responsibility for their learning.

Implementing data-driven personalization in education does require careful planning and consideration. Privacy and security are paramount when handling student data. Schools and educators must adhere to strict data protection regulations and ensure that sensitive information is safeguarded against unauthorized access. Transparency is also crucial; students and their families should be informed about the types of data being collected, how it will be used, and the benefits it offers.

Another challenge lies in the potential for data overload. With so much information available, educators must focus on identifying the most relevant data points that will genuinely inform instructional decisions. Professional development and training are essential for teachers to develop the skills needed to interpret data effectively and integrate it into their teaching practices. By equipping educators with these skills, schools can ensure that data-driven personalization becomes a seamless and valuable component of the educational experience.

The success of data-driven personalization also hinges on the availability and quality of digital tools and platforms. Educational technology that supports data analysis and personalized learning must be user-friendly and adaptable to different learning contexts. These tools should facilitate the collection, processing, and presentation of data in a way that is accessible and actionable for educators, students, and parents alike.

Despite these challenges, the potential of data-driven personalization to transform education is immense. By addressing individual learning needs, this approach promotes equity and inclusion, ensuring that all students have access to high-quality, personalized education. It empowers educators to move beyond a one-size-fits-all approach and embrace a more dynamic and responsive teaching model.

Data-driven personalization represents a significant shift in how education is delivered and experienced. As schools and educators continue to explore and implement this approach, they are paving the way for a more inclusive and effective educational system. By harnessing the power of data, we can create learning environments that celebrate diversity, honor individual differences, and unlock the full potential of every student.

In essence, data-driven personalization is not merely about using technology but about reimagining the learning experience. It is a call to action for educators to embrace innovation and creativity, to think beyond traditional boundaries, and to create a future where every student has the opportunity to succeed. As we continue this journey, we remain committed to the belief that education should be as unique as the individuals it serves.

Adaptive Learning Algorithms and Techniques

Adaptive learning algorithms have emerged as powerful tools in modern education, offering customized experiences that cater to individual learning styles and paces. By utilizing data-driven insights, these algorithms dynamically adjust educational content, ensuring that each student receives the most relevant and effective instruction. Understanding the fundamentals of adaptive learning can significantly enhance the educational journey for both students and educators.

At its core, adaptive learning is about personalization. Unlike traditional educational models, which often adopt a one-size-fits-all approach, adaptive techniques focus on tailoring the learning experience to the unique needs of each student. This customization is achieved through sophisticated algorithms that analyze a student's performance in real-time, identifying areas of strength and weakness. As a result, students receive content that is neither too easy nor too challenging, maintaining optimal engagement and motivation.

Consider a student struggling with fractions in a math class. Traditional methods might require the entire class to move on to the next topic, but adaptive learning systems can identify this student's difficulty and provide additional resources or exercises specifically targeting their gaps in understanding. By addressing these issues promptly, adaptive learning ensures that no student is left behind, promoting mastery of foundational concepts before proceeding to more complex topics.

One of the key advantages of adaptive learning algorithms is their ability to provide immediate feedback. As students interact with the material, the system continuously monitors their progress, offering instant responses to their inputs. This real-time feedback loop not only helps students correct mistakes promptly but also reinforces their understanding by providing explanations and alternative approaches. Such immediate reinforcement is crucial in solidifying knowledge and preventing misconceptions from taking root.

For educators, adaptive learning offers valuable insights into student performance. Teachers can access detailed analytics that highlight trends, pinpoint common challenges, and identify students who may require additional support. Armed with this information, educators can make informed decisions about instructional strategies, tailor interventions to specific needs, and allocate resources more effectively. By leveraging adaptive technologies, teachers become facilitators of personalized learning experiences, guiding students on their individual paths to success.

Implementing adaptive learning algorithms requires careful consideration of technological infrastructure and pedagogical goals. Schools and institutions must invest in robust digital platforms capable of supporting adaptive systems. These platforms should be user-friendly, ensuring that both students and educators can navigate them with ease. Additionally, it's essential to align adaptive learning initiatives with curricular objectives, ensuring that the technology complements and enhances traditional teaching methods rather than replacing them.

Training and professional development are crucial components of successful adaptive learning implementation. Educators must be equipped with the skills to effectively integrate adaptive technologies into their teaching practices. This includes understanding how to interpret data analytics, designing adaptive learning paths, and providing personalized support to students. By investing in teacher training, schools can ensure that adaptive learning becomes an integral and effective part of the educational landscape.

Despite the many benefits, there are challenges associated with adaptive learning algorithms. One potential concern is the risk of over-reliance on technology at the expense of human interaction. Education is not solely about content delivery; it is also about fostering relationships, developing critical thinking skills, and nurturing creativity. To address this, adaptive learning should be used as a tool to enhance, rather than replace, the human elements of teaching and learning. Balancing technology with personal interaction ensures a holistic educational experience that prepares students for the complexities of the modern world.

Another challenge is data privacy. Adaptive learning systems rely on collecting and analyzing student data to function effectively. It is imperative to implement stringent data protection measures to safeguard student information from unauthorized access. Transparency about data collection practices and obtaining informed consent from students and their guardians are essential steps in building trust and ensuring ethical use of technology in education.

The potential of adaptive learning algorithms to transform education is immense. By offering personalized, data-driven learning experiences, these systems empower students to take ownership of their education, fostering engagement and motivation. For educators, adaptive learning provides a powerful tool to enhance instructional effectiveness, improve learning outcomes, and create inclusive environments where every student can thrive.

As we continue to explore and refine adaptive learning techniques, it is crucial to remain mindful of the overarching goal: to provide meaningful, equitable, and accessible education for all. By harnessing the power of adaptive learning in thoughtful and intentional ways, we can create a future where education is not just about acquiring knowledge, but about unlocking the full potential of every learner. Through collaboration, innovation, and a commitment to continuous improvement, adaptive learning can be a catalyst for positive change in education, paving the way for a brighter future for students worldwide.

Tailoring Educational Content to Individual Needs

Tailoring educational content to individual needs is an approach that recognizes the diverse ways in which students learn and process information. This method prioritizes the customization of learning experiences to optimize engagement, comprehension, and retention. As education continues to evolve, the importance of personalized learning becomes increasingly evident, offering a pathway to more effective and inclusive educational environments.

Imagine a classroom filled with students who each bring their own unique backgrounds, interests, and learning styles. Traditional educational models often struggle to accommodate such diversity, resulting in some students thriving while others fall behind. Tailoring educational content seeks to bridge this gap by ensuring that each student receives instruction that is relevant and accessible to them. This personalized approach fosters a deeper connection to the material, making learning more meaningful and enjoyable.

To effectively tailor educational content, it is essential to first understand the individual needs of each student. This understanding can be achieved through a combination of assessments, observations, and dialogues. Teachers can gather insights into students' learning preferences, strengths, and areas for improvement. By building a comprehensive profile of each learner, educators can design targeted interventions that address specific needs and leverage individual strengths.

One practical method for tailoring content is through differentiated instruction. This technique involves modifying the curriculum to offer multiple pathways for students to engage with the material. For instance, a history lesson could be presented through a variety of formats, such as written texts, interactive timelines, multimedia presentations, or role-playing activities. By providing options that cater to different learning styles, teachers can ensure that all students have the opportunity to grasp the concepts being taught.

Another key aspect of tailoring educational content is the use of formative assessments. These assessments are conducted throughout the learning process and provide valuable feedback on student progress. By analyzing assessment data, educators can identify patterns and trends that inform instructional adjustments. For example, if a student consistently struggles with a particular concept, the teacher can offer additional resources or alternative explanations to reinforce understanding. This iterative process allows for continuous refinement of teaching strategies, ensuring that instruction remains aligned with student needs.

Technology plays a pivotal role in facilitating personalized learning. Digital platforms can provide adaptive learning experiences that adjust to a student's performance in real-time. These platforms often include interactive exercises, quizzes, and tutorials that are tailored to the learner's level of proficiency. As students engage with the content, the system adapts, offering more challenging tasks as they progress or revisiting foundational concepts as needed. This dynamic approach not only enhances learning outcomes but also boosts student confidence and motivation.

Collaboration between educators, students, and parents is crucial in tailoring educational content effectively. Teachers should maintain open lines of communication with students, encouraging them to express their preferences and feedback. By involving students in the decision-making process, educators empower them to take ownership of their learning journey. Additionally, engaging parents as partners in education provides valuable insights and support, reinforcing the connection between home and school environments.

While tailoring educational content offers numerous benefits, it also presents challenges. One potential obstacle is the time and effort required to design personalized learning experiences. Educators must balance the demands of individualized instruction with other responsibilities, such as administrative tasks and classroom management. To address this, schools can provide professional development opportunities that equip teachers with the skills and resources needed to implement personalized learning effectively. Support from colleagues and access to collaborative planning tools can also alleviate the workload and foster a culture of shared responsibility.

Moreover, it is important to recognize that personalization does not imply isolation. While tailoring content to individual needs is essential, fostering a sense of community and collaboration among students remains a priority. Group activities, peer-to-peer learning, and collaborative projects can complement personalized instruction, promoting social interaction and the development of essential interpersonal skills.

Tailoring educational content to individual needs is a transformative approach that has the potential to revolutionize the way we educate students. By acknowledging and embracing the diversity of learners, educators can create environments where every student feels valued and supported. This approach not only enhances academic achievement but also nurtures a love for learning that extends beyond the classroom.

As we continue to refine and expand personalized learning strategies, the focus should remain on creating equitable and inclusive educational opportunities for all students. Through innovation, collaboration, and a commitment to continuous improvement, we can build a future where education is truly tailored to meet the needs of every learner.

The Impact of AI on Personalized Learning

In a world where technology continuously transforms various facets of life, education stands at the forefront of this digital revolution. The integration of advanced technologies has opened doors to new possibilities, particularly in the realm of personalized learning. By leveraging the capabilities of AI, educators can now tailor educational experiences to meet the unique needs of each student, paving the way for a more effective and engaging learning journey.

Imagine a classroom where each student embarks on a personalized educational path, guided by insights derived from data-driven analysis. The role of AI in this transformation is pivotal, as it enables the customization of learning experiences in ways that were previously unattainable. By analyzing a wealth of data, AI systems can identify patterns and trends, allowing educators to develop targeted strategies that address individual learning styles and preferences.

One of the most significant impacts of AI on personalized learning is its ability to provide real-time feedback. As students interact with educational content, AI systems continuously monitor their progress, offering immediate insights into their strengths and areas for improvement. This instantaneous feedback helps students understand concepts more deeply and adjust their learning strategies accordingly. For educators, this means having access to detailed analytics that can inform instructional decisions, making teaching more responsive and adaptive.

Consider a student who struggles with mathematics. Traditional methods might overlook their specific challenges, but AI-driven platforms can pinpoint the exact areas where they need support. By providing tailored exercises and resources, these systems ensure that students receive the assistance they need to overcome obstacles and build a solid foundation in the subject. As a result, students experience a sense of achievement and confidence, fostering a positive attitude toward learning.

Moreover, AI enhances personalized learning by offering diverse and engaging content. Through intelligent algorithms, AI can curate a wealth of resources, including videos, articles, and interactive simulations, that cater to various learning preferences. For visual learners, AI might select multimedia presentations, while auditory learners might benefit from podcasts or audio explanations. This diversity not only enriches the learning experience but also ensures that each student can engage with content in a way that resonates with them.

The benefits of AI in personalized learning extend beyond individual academic performance. By creating a more inclusive educational environment, AI has the potential to bridge gaps and promote equity. Students with special educational needs, for example, can benefit from AI-driven tools that provide customized support and accommodations. Whether it's through speech recognition software, text-to-speech applications, or adaptive learning platforms, AI empowers students to learn at their own pace and in their own way, leveling the playing field for all learners.

Despite the advantages, integrating AI into personalized learning comes with its challenges. Educators must navigate concerns related to data privacy and security, ensuring that student information is protected from unauthorized access. Transparent communication about data collection practices and obtaining consent from students and their families are crucial steps in building trust and maintaining ethical standards.

Additionally, there is a risk that an over-reliance on AI could diminish the human element of education. While AI can provide valuable insights and resources, the role of educators remains essential. Teachers are not only facilitators of knowledge but also mentors and role models who inspire and motivate students. Balancing the use of AI with personal interaction ensures that education remains a holistic and enriching experience.

To maximize the potential of AI in personalized learning, it is important to invest in professional development for educators. Training programs that equip teachers with the skills to effectively integrate AI tools into their teaching practices are vital. By fostering a culture of collaboration and innovation, schools can create an environment where AI and educators work in harmony to enhance the learning experience.

As we continue to explore the possibilities of AI in education, it is essential to maintain a focus on the ultimate goal: to provide meaningful and impactful learning experiences for all students. By embracing AI's potential while remaining mindful of its limitations, educators can harness this powerful tool to transform education for the better.

The impact of AI on personalized learning is profound, offering new opportunities for customization, engagement, and accessibility. As we navigate this evolving landscape, the commitment to continuous improvement and ethical considerations will guide us in creating a future where education is tailored to the needs of every learner.

Case Studies: Success Stories in Personalized Education

Across the globe, personalized education has been making significant strides, revolutionizing the ways in which learning is approached and delivered. These transformations aren't merely theoretical; they manifest in real-world success stories that highlight the impact of tailoring education to fit the diverse needs of learners. From rural communities to bustling urban centers, case studies illuminate how personalized education can foster engagement, enhance comprehension, and drive academic achievement.

In the picturesque town of Walla Walla, Washington, a public school embarked on a journey to redefine its educational strategy by focusing on individual student growth. The school introduced a comprehensive personalized learning program that utilized project-based learning and student-driven inquiry. Teachers were trained to act as facilitators, guiding students in setting their own learning objectives and selecting projects aligned with their interests. This approach not only empowered students to take charge of their education but also led to a remarkable improvement in student motivation and performance. Within two years, standardized test scores rose significantly, and the dropout rate plummeted. Students reported feeling more valued and engaged, attributing their success to the newfound sense of ownership over their learning journey.

In another inspiring example, a rural school district in Kenya faced the challenge of limited resources and a high student-to-teacher ratio. Determined to provide quality education, the district implemented a personalized learning model that leveraged technology to deliver customized instruction. Each student was provided with a tablet loaded with educational software tailored to their learning level. The program included interactive lessons, quizzes, and tutorials that adapted based on student performance. Teachers received training to interpret data generated by the software, allowing them to provide targeted support and interventions. The results were astounding; within a year, literacy rates soared, and students demonstrated significant gains in math and science. This success story underscores the potential of personalized education to bridge educational gaps, even in resource-constrained environments.

A third case study takes us to Helsinki, Finland, where a primary school embraced a holistic approach to personalized education. Recognizing that learning extends beyond academics, the school integrated social-emotional learning and mindfulness practices into its curriculum. Students were encouraged to set personal goals, reflect on their progress, and develop self-regulation skills. Teachers collaborated with students to co-create learning plans that balanced academic rigor with emotional well-being. This inclusive approach led to a marked improvement in student behavior, communication skills, and overall school climate. Parents and educators noted that students became more resilient and better equipped to navigate challenges, both inside and outside the classroom.

The innovative efforts in New York City's Pathways in Technology Early College High School (P-TECH) showcase yet another dimension of personalized education. Established to address the skills gap in the technology sector, P-TECH offers a unique model that combines high school, college, and career training. Students engage in a personalized curriculum that aligns with industry standards, gaining both a high school diploma and an associate degree in technology. The program's success lies in its strong partnerships with local colleges and tech companies, providing students with mentorship, internships, and real-world experience. Since its inception, P-TECH has achieved impressive graduation rates, with many students securing employment in the tech industry immediately upon completion. This model exemplifies how personalized education can prepare students for the workforce, equipping them with the skills and knowledge needed to thrive in a rapidly evolving job market.

In the bustling city of Bangalore, India, an international school embraced personalized education through a student-centered approach to language learning. Recognizing that language acquisition is unique to each learner, the school implemented a program that allowed students to choose the languages they wished to study and set personalized learning goals. Teachers utilized a variety of resources, including multimedia, interactive applications, and cultural immersion activities, to cater to individual preferences and learning styles. The program's flexibility and adaptability resulted in higher language proficiency levels and increased student enthusiasm for language learning. Students developed a deeper appreciation for different cultures, enhancing their global awareness and communication skills.

These case studies illustrate the transformative power of personalized education across diverse contexts and challenges. While each story is unique, common themes emerge: the importance of student agency, the role of technology in facilitating personalized learning, and the need for supportive, trained educators who can guide and mentor students on their educational journeys. Personalized education is not a one-size-fits-all solution; rather, it is a dynamic and evolving approach that requires ongoing collaboration and innovation.

For educators and policymakers seeking to implement personalized education, these success stories offer valuable lessons. It is essential to create a culture that prioritizes student agency and fosters a growth mindset. Educators must be equipped with the tools and training needed to effectively facilitate personalized learning, while technology should be leveraged to enhance, rather than replace, human interaction. Collaboration with parents, communities, and industry partners can further enrich the learning experience, providing students with diverse opportunities and perspectives.

As these case studies demonstrate, personalized education has the potential to transform not only individual student outcomes but also entire educational systems. By embracing personalization, we can create learning environments that nurture curiosity, inspire innovation, and empower students to reach their full potential. Through creativity, commitment, and collaboration, personalized education can pave the way for a brighter and more equitable future for learners worldwide.

Chapter 4: Enhancing Educator Effectiveness with EdTech

Professional Development and Training for Educators

Professional development and training for educators are crucial components in the journey toward creating a dynamic and responsive educational environment. As the landscape of education continues to evolve, driven by technological advancements and the increasing demand for personalized learning, the need for educators to adapt and grow becomes more pressing. Effective professional development empowers teachers, equipping them with the skills and knowledge necessary to meet the diverse needs of their students and to foster an engaging and inclusive classroom experience.

Imagine a teacher entering a bustling classroom, a place where each student reflects a unique blend of abilities, interests, and learning styles. To navigate this complexity, educators require a robust set of tools and strategies, honed through targeted professional development. This ongoing process involves not only acquiring new skills but also reflecting on existing practices, collaborating with peers, and embracing innovative teaching methodologies. By committing to lifelong learning, educators can remain at the forefront of educational best practices, ensuring that their students receive the highest quality of instruction.

One of the primary goals of professional development is to enhance instructional effectiveness. Workshops, seminars, and courses provide educators with opportunities to explore new pedagogical approaches and technologies that can enrich their teaching. Whether it's learning to integrate digital tools into the curriculum or adopting differentiated instruction techniques, these experiences broaden teachers' repertoires and encourage experimentation in the classroom. For example, a mathematics teacher might attend a workshop on project-based learning, discovering how to create real-world scenarios that make abstract concepts tangible for students. By applying these insights, the teacher can transform the classroom into an interactive and stimulating learning environment.

Collaboration plays a pivotal role in professional development, offering educators a platform to share experiences, exchange ideas, and learn from one another. Professional learning communities (PLCs) are an effective way to foster collaboration, bringing together teachers with common goals and interests. Within these communities, educators can engage in meaningful dialogue, analyze student work, and collectively solve instructional challenges. This collaborative process not only enhances individual practice but also builds a supportive network that promotes collective growth and innovation.

Moreover, professional development should be personalized to address the specific needs and goals of each educator. Just as students benefit from tailored instruction, teachers thrive when their professional learning is customized to align with their career stage, subject area, and teaching context. Personalized professional development might include mentorship programs, where novice teachers receive guidance and support from experienced colleagues, or self-directed learning opportunities, where teachers pursue areas of interest through online courses or conferences. By taking ownership of their professional growth, educators can focus on developing the skills most relevant to their practice and aspirations.

Incorporating reflective practice is another essential element of professional development. Reflection encourages educators to critically examine their teaching, identify areas for improvement, and set goals for future growth. This process can be facilitated through journaling, peer observations, or video recordings of classroom instruction. By engaging in reflection, teachers can gain a deeper understanding of their instructional strategies, student interactions, and classroom dynamics. This self-awareness empowers educators to make informed decisions about their practice, fostering a culture of continuous improvement.

While professional development offers numerous benefits, it is not without its challenges. One common obstacle is finding the time and resources to engage in meaningful learning experiences. Teachers often juggle multiple responsibilities, making it difficult to prioritize professional growth. To address this, schools and districts can create supportive structures that prioritize and allocate time for professional development. Flexible scheduling, dedicated professional development days, and access to online learning platforms are just a few ways to make professional development more accessible and manageable for educators.

Evaluating the impact of professional development is also crucial to ensure its effectiveness. Schools should implement mechanisms to assess whether professional learning initiatives translate into improved teaching practices and student outcomes. This evaluation process might involve collecting feedback from participants, analyzing changes in instructional strategies, or examining student performance data. By assessing the impact of professional development, educators and administrators can make data-informed decisions about future learning opportunities, ensuring that they align with the needs and goals of the school community.

Professional development and training for educators are essential components of a thriving educational ecosystem. By investing in the growth and development of teachers, schools create a culture of excellence that benefits both educators and students. As teachers deepen their expertise, embrace innovation, and collaborate with peers, they become better equipped to meet the challenges of an ever-changing educational landscape. Through dedication to lifelong learning, educators can inspire and empower the next generation of learners, fostering a brighter future for all.

Collaborative Tools for Teacher and Student Interaction

In the contemporary educational landscape, the integration of collaborative tools has become a linchpin in fostering meaningful interactions between teachers and students. These tools, which range from digital platforms to interactive applications, have transformed the traditional classroom setting, enabling seamless communication and collaboration that transcend geographical and temporal barriers. As educators and students navigate this evolving terrain, understanding the diverse array of available tools and their effective implementation becomes paramount.

Imagine a classroom where communication is not confined to face-to-face interactions during set hours. Instead, it extends beyond these limitations, allowing for continuous engagement and support. Collaborative tools such as learning management systems (LMS), video conferencing software, and interactive whiteboards make this possible.

These technologies facilitate a dynamic flow of information, enabling teachers to share resources, assignments, and feedback with students in real time. Students, in turn, can collaborate with peers, participate in discussions, and seek clarification on complex concepts, all within a virtual space that mirrors the collaborative nature of a physical classroom.

One of the most widely adopted collaborative tools in education is the learning management system. Platforms like Moodle, Canvas, and Google Classroom provide a centralized hub where educators can organize course content, administer assessments, and track student progress. These systems offer a suite of features that support both synchronous and asynchronous learning. For instance, teachers can post lecture recordings, create discussion forums, and schedule quizzes, allowing students to access course materials at their own pace. This flexibility is particularly beneficial for accommodating diverse learning styles and schedules, ensuring that all students have equal opportunities to engage with the curriculum.

Video conferencing software, such as Zoom and Microsoft Teams, has also become an indispensable tool for facilitating live interactions between teachers and students. These platforms support virtual classrooms, where participants can engage in real-time discussions, group activities, and presentations. Features like screen sharing and breakout rooms enhance the interactive nature of these sessions, allowing teachers to deliver content dynamically and students to collaborate in small groups. The ability to record sessions provides an additional layer of accessibility, enabling students to revisit lessons and reinforce their understanding outside of class time.

Interactive whiteboards and digital collaboration spaces, such as Jamboard and Miro, offer creative avenues for teachers and students to co-create content. These tools simulate a physical whiteboard, allowing participants to draw, annotate, and brainstorm ideas collaboratively. Teachers can use them to visualize complex concepts, facilitate problem-solving sessions, or conduct interactive lessons that encourage active participation. For students, these platforms provide an opportunity to engage in hands-on learning, develop critical thinking skills, and express their ideas visually.

In addition to these tools, social learning platforms like Edmodo and Piazza provide a forum for peer-to-peer interaction and collaborative learning. These platforms function as social networks for education, where students can form study groups, share resources, and participate in discussions outside of the classroom. By fostering a sense of community and collaboration, these tools encourage students to take an active role in their learning journey, enhancing their engagement and motivation.

While collaborative tools offer numerous benefits, their successful implementation requires thoughtful planning and consideration. Educators must ensure that these tools align with their pedagogical goals and enhance, rather than hinder, the learning experience. This involves selecting tools that are user-friendly, accessible, and appropriate for the age and skill level of the students. Moreover, teachers should receive adequate training and support to effectively integrate these technologies into their teaching practices.

Equity and accessibility are also critical considerations when implementing collaborative tools. Schools must strive to provide all students with the necessary resources and infrastructure to access digital platforms, including reliable internet connectivity and devices. Ensuring that collaborative tools are accessible to students with diverse needs, including those with disabilities, is essential for creating an inclusive educational environment.

As educators and students become more adept at using collaborative tools, the potential for innovative teaching and learning approaches continues to grow. These tools open the door to project-based learning, flipped classrooms, and remote collaborations that transcend traditional boundaries. By harnessing the power of technology, educators can create immersive and interactive learning experiences that prepare students for the demands of an increasingly interconnected world.

The integration of collaborative tools for teacher and student interaction is a transformative development in education, offering new possibilities for engagement, collaboration, and personalization. As we continue to explore the potential of these technologies, the focus should remain on creating meaningful and impactful learning experiences that empower both educators and students. Through thoughtful implementation and ongoing support, collaborative tools can serve as a catalyst for positive change, enriching the educational journey and fostering a culture of lifelong learning.

Utilizing Analytics to Improve Teaching Practices

The advent of data analytics in education has ushered in a new era of insight-driven teaching practices. By harnessing the power of analytics, educators can gain a deeper understanding of student performance, identify trends, and tailor their instructional strategies to meet the diverse needs of their learners. This chapter delves into the practical application of analytics in education, offering actionable advice for beginners eager to integrate data-informed decision-making into their teaching.

Imagine a classroom where every student's progress is meticulously tracked, offering a comprehensive view of their strengths and areas for improvement. This is the promise of educational analytics—a transformative tool that empowers educators to move beyond intuition and anecdotal evidence. By analyzing data from assessments, attendance records, and engagement metrics, teachers can craft personalized learning experiences that foster academic growth and student success.

To begin utilizing analytics in teaching, it's essential to establish clear objectives. Identifying what you want to measure and why provides a solid foundation for data collection and interpretation. For instance, if the goal is to enhance reading comprehension, consider tracking metrics such as time spent on reading assignments, quiz scores, and participation in reading discussions. By focusing on specific objectives, educators can ensure that their data-gathering efforts remain targeted and relevant.

Data collection is the next crucial step in the analytics process. Many educational institutions employ software systems that automatically gather and organize data, simplifying the task for teachers. Learning management systems (LMS) and student information systems (SIS) are valuable resources for accessing data related to student performance, attendance, and engagement. For those without access to such systems, traditional methods like surveys, observational notes, and manual record-keeping can also provide valuable insights. The key is consistency in data collection to establish reliable trends and patterns over time.

Once data is collected, the analysis begins. This involves examining the data to identify meaningful patterns and correlations. For newcomers to analytics, it might be helpful to start with basic statistical methods, such as calculating averages, identifying outliers, or tracking progress over time. Visualization tools like graphs and charts can make it easier to interpret data and communicate findings. For example, a line graph depicting student performance over a semester can highlight areas where additional support or intervention may be needed. By visualizing data, educators can quickly pinpoint trends that warrant attention.

Analytics becomes truly impactful when used to inform instructional decisions. Consider a scenario where data reveals that a significant number of students are struggling with a particular math concept. Armed with this insight, a teacher might decide to revisit the topic using different instructional approaches, such as incorporating hands-on activities or offering supplementary resources. By aligning teaching strategies with data-driven insights, educators can create a more responsive and effective learning environment.

Feedback loops are an integral component of utilizing analytics in education. Regularly communicating insights derived from data to students fosters a culture of transparency and collaboration. By sharing data with students, educators can empower them to take an active role in their learning journey. For instance, a teacher might discuss a student's progress in a one-on-one conference, highlighting areas of improvement and setting goals for the future. This dialogue not only enhances student engagement but also encourages a growth mindset.

Professional development plays a vital role in equipping educators with the skills needed to leverage analytics effectively. Training sessions, workshops, and online courses can provide valuable guidance on data interpretation, analysis techniques, and the integration of analytics into teaching practices. Collaboration with colleagues can also enhance data literacy, as teachers share insights and strategies for incorporating analytics into their classrooms. A supportive community of practice fosters an environment where educators can learn from one another and continuously refine their approach to data-informed teaching.

While analytics offers numerous benefits, it is important to remain mindful of potential challenges. Data privacy and security are paramount, and educators must adhere to regulations and best practices to protect student information. Additionally, over-reliance on data can lead to a reductionist view of student capabilities. It's crucial to balance quantitative insights with qualitative observations, ensuring that the holistic nature of education is preserved.

Utilizing analytics to improve teaching practices is a journey that combines curiosity, exploration, and reflection. By embracing data-informed decision-making, educators can create a more personalized and impactful learning experience for their students. As teachers become more adept at interpreting and applying data, they unlock new possibilities for fostering academic success and nurturing a lifelong love of learning. Through thoughtful implementation and a commitment to continuous growth, analytics can serve as a powerful ally in the pursuit of educational excellence.

Streamlining Administrative Tasks with Technology

Administrative tasks, often viewed as the backbone of educational institutions, are crucial in ensuring that the daily operations of schools run smoothly. However, these tasks can be time-consuming and labor-intensive, detracting from the core mission of education—teaching and learning. Enter the realm of technology, which offers a plethora of solutions designed to streamline administrative processes, allowing educators and administrators to focus more on what truly matters: student success.

Consider a bustling school office, where papers pile high and staff juggle multiple responsibilities, from managing student records to coordinating schedules. Traditional methods of handling these tasks can be cumbersome and error-prone. Technology, however, has transformed these processes, offering tools that enhance efficiency and accuracy. By digitizing administrative functions, schools can reduce the burden on staff, improve data management, and create a more organized and effective educational environment.

One of the most significant advancements in streamlining administrative tasks is the use of student information systems (SIS). These comprehensive platforms centralize data management, allowing schools to efficiently handle student enrollment, attendance, grades, and more. By consolidating information into a single digital system, SIS platforms eliminate the need for physical paperwork and enable quick access to student records. This not only saves time but also reduces the risk of data loss or duplication. For instance, when a teacher needs to update a student's academic record, they can do so with just a few clicks, ensuring that information is accurate and up-to-date.

The automation of routine tasks is another way technology enhances administrative efficiency. Tools like automated attendance systems use biometric or RFID technology to track student presence, eliminating the need for manual roll calls. Similarly, automated scheduling software can generate timetables and allocate resources based on predefined criteria, reducing the complexity of managing school calendars. By automating these processes, schools can minimize human error and free up valuable time for staff to focus on more strategic initiatives.

Communication, a vital component of school administration, also benefits from technological advancements. Platforms that offer integrated communication solutions, such as email, messaging, and notifications, streamline interactions between staff, students, and parents. These platforms enable instant communication, ensuring that important information is disseminated quickly and efficiently. For example, in the event of a schedule change, administrators can send automated alerts to all affected parties, minimizing confusion and ensuring that everyone is informed in real-time.

Financial management, often a complex aspect of school administration, is also simplified through technology. Financial software solutions facilitate budget planning, expense tracking, and financial reporting, providing schools with greater control and oversight of their finances. These tools can generate detailed reports and analytics, offering insights into spending patterns and financial health. By streamlining financial processes, schools can ensure fiscal responsibility and allocate resources more effectively to support educational goals.

Despite the numerous benefits, integrating technology into administrative tasks requires careful planning and implementation. Selecting the right tools that align with the specific needs and goals of the institution is crucial. Schools should consider factors such as user-friendliness, scalability, and compatibility with existing systems when evaluating technological solutions. Additionally, training and support for staff are essential to ensure successful adoption and utilization of new tools. Providing professional development opportunities and ongoing technical support can help staff feel confident and competent in using technology to streamline administrative functions.

Data security and privacy are paramount when implementing technological solutions in schools. Educational institutions must adhere to strict regulations and best practices to protect sensitive information. This involves implementing robust security measures, such as encryption and access controls, to safeguard data from unauthorized access or breaches. By prioritizing data security, schools can build trust with students, parents, and staff, ensuring that information is handled responsibly and ethically.

As technology continues to evolve, so too does the potential for further streamlining administrative tasks in education. Emerging technologies, such as artificial intelligence and machine learning, offer exciting possibilities for automating complex processes and providing predictive insights. For example, AI-driven analytics can forecast enrollment trends or identify patterns in student performance, enabling data-informed decision-making. By staying informed about technological advancements and exploring innovative solutions, schools can remain agile and responsive to changing administrative needs.

The integration of technology into administrative tasks is a transformative development that offers numerous benefits for educational institutions. By streamlining processes, improving efficiency, and enhancing data management, technology empowers schools to focus on their primary mission: delivering high-quality education. With thoughtful implementation and a commitment to continuous improvement, technology can serve as a powerful ally in the pursuit of educational excellence, creating a more organized, effective, and future-ready school environment.

Building a Community of Practice Among Educators

Creating a thriving community of practice among educators is a powerful strategy that can enhance professional growth, foster collaboration, and ultimately lead to improved educational outcomes. By forming a network of educators who share common goals and interests, a community of practice provides a supportive environment where teachers can exchange ideas, share experiences, and collaboratively solve challenges. This chapter delves into the essence of building such a community, offering practical advice for beginners eager to embark on this transformative journey.

Picture a group of educators gathered in a lively discussion, each bringing their unique perspectives and experiences to the table. This dynamic interaction is the heart of a community of practice—a space where learning is both social and collaborative. Within this community, educators have the opportunity to engage in meaningful conversations, explore innovative teaching strategies, and reflect on their practices. The collective wisdom of the group enriches each member's professional journey, fostering a sense of belonging and shared purpose.

The first step in building a community of practice is identifying a shared domain of interest. This domain serves as the focal point around which the community coalesces, guiding discussions and activities. It could be a specific subject area, such as mathematics or science, or a broader theme, like student engagement or technology integration. By defining the domain, educators can attract like-minded individuals who are passionate about similar topics, creating a cohesive and focused community.

Once the domain is established, finding a core group of committed participants is crucial. These individuals, often referred to as the community's "core group," play a pivotal role in initiating and sustaining the community's activities. They are responsible for organizing meetings, facilitating discussions, and maintaining momentum. The core group should consist of educators who are enthusiastic about the domain and willing to invest time and energy into nurturing the community.

Creating a welcoming and inclusive environment is essential for fostering engagement and participation. Encouraging open communication and valuing diverse perspectives ensures that all members feel respected and heard. Establishing ground rules for interactions, such as active listening and constructive feedback, can help create a positive and supportive atmosphere. By fostering a culture of trust and mutual respect, the community can become a safe space for educators to share challenges, celebrate successes, and learn from one another.

Regular meetings are a cornerstone of a successful community of practice. Whether held in person or virtually, these gatherings provide a structured opportunity for members to connect, share insights, and collaborate on projects. The format of meetings can vary, ranging from informal discussions and workshops to presentations and guest speakers. It's important to tailor the meeting format to the preferences and needs of the community, ensuring that sessions are engaging and relevant. Incorporating a mix of activities, such as brainstorming sessions, case studies, and peer observations, can keep meetings dynamic and interactive. In addition to meetings, digital platforms offer a valuable means of communication and collaboration between gatherings. Online forums, social media groups, and collaborative tools provide a space for ongoing dialogue, resource sharing, and collaborative projects. These platforms enable members to stay connected, exchange ideas, and access a wealth of resources at their convenience. By leveraging digital tools, the community can extend its reach and impact, accommodating diverse schedules and geographical locations.

Reflection and evaluation are integral to the growth and sustainability of a community of practice. Regularly assessing the community's activities and outcomes allows members to identify areas of success and opportunities for improvement. This process can involve collecting feedback from participants, reviewing meeting attendance and engagement, and assessing the impact of the community on professional practice. By reflecting on the community's progress, educators can make informed decisions about future directions and activities, ensuring that the community remains responsive to the evolving needs of its members.

While building a community of practice requires dedication and effort, the benefits are well worth the investment. Educators who participate in such communities often report increased motivation, enhanced teaching practices, and a greater sense of professional fulfillment. The collaborative nature of the community fosters a culture of continuous learning and innovation, empowering educators to stay informed about current trends and best practices. Moreover, the supportive network of peers provides encouragement and inspiration, helping educators navigate challenges and celebrate achievements.

In conclusion, building a community of practice among educators is a transformative endeavor that holds the potential to enrich professional lives and elevate educational experiences. By fostering collaboration, sharing knowledge, and supporting one another, educators can create a vibrant and dynamic community that thrives on collective wisdom and shared passion. Through thoughtful planning, commitment, and a spirit of collaboration, a community of practice can become a powerful force for positive change, shaping the future of education for the better.

Chapter 5: EdTech and Student Engagement

Strategies for Increasing Student Participation

Increasing student participation in the classroom is a critical component of an effective teaching strategy. Participation not only enhances student engagement but also fosters a deeper understanding of the subject matter, encourages critical thinking, and builds communication skills. To achieve meaningful participation, educators must employ a variety of strategies that cater to the diverse needs and learning styles of their students. This chapter provides practical advice for teachers looking to create an inclusive and participatory classroom environment.

Begin by setting a foundation of trust and respect, essential elements for encouraging student participation. When students feel safe and valued, they are more likely to engage actively in class discussions and activities. Establishing clear expectations and guidelines for participation can help create a structured and supportive environment. Encourage students to express their thoughts and opinions without fear of judgment, and emphasize the importance of listening to and respecting diverse perspectives. By fostering a culture of open communication, educators can create a classroom atmosphere where all students feel comfortable contributing.

Varying instructional methods is another effective strategy for increasing student participation. Different students thrive in different learning environments, so incorporating a mix of teaching techniques can engage a broader range of learners. For example, lectures can be interspersed with interactive activities such as group discussions, debates, or role-plays. These activities not only break the monotony of traditional instruction but also provide students with opportunities to apply their knowledge in dynamic and collaborative settings. Additionally, incorporating technology, such as educational apps or online discussion forums, can appeal to tech-savvy students and encourage participation beyond the classroom.

Active learning techniques, such as think-pair-share or jigsaw activities, are particularly effective in promoting student participation. These methods require students to engage with the material actively, collaborate with peers, and articulate their understanding. In a think-pair-share activity, for instance, students first consider a question individually, then discuss their thoughts with a partner, and finally share their conclusions with the class. This structured approach ensures that all students have the opportunity to participate and contributes to a richer classroom discussion.

Differentiating instruction to accommodate diverse learning styles and abilities is crucial for maximizing student participation. By providing multiple ways for students to engage with the content, educators can ensure that all students have the opportunity to participate meaningfully. This might involve offering choices in how students demonstrate their understanding, such as through written assignments, presentations, or creative projects. By allowing students to choose the format that best suits their strengths and interests, teachers can increase motivation and participation.

Questioning techniques also play a crucial role in fostering student participation. Crafting open-ended questions that encourage critical thinking and exploration can stimulate richer classroom discussions. Instead of asking questions that elicit simple yes or no answers, pose questions that require students to analyze, synthesize, and evaluate information. For example, rather than asking, "Did you like the story?" consider asking, "What themes in the story resonated with you, and why?" By encouraging deeper reflection, educators can prompt students to engage more thoughtfully and meaningfully with the material.

Providing opportunities for student-led activities can empower students and increase participation. Allowing students to take on leadership roles, such as facilitating a discussion or leading a group project, can boost confidence and encourage active engagement. When students are given the responsibility to guide their peers, they often take ownership of their learning and become more invested in the process. Additionally, student-led activities provide an opportunity for students to develop leadership and communication skills, which are valuable both inside and outside the classroom.

Feedback and recognition are powerful motivators for student participation. Acknowledging and valuing students' contributions can reinforce positive behavior and encourage continued engagement. Providing constructive feedback that highlights strengths and offers guidance for improvement can help students build confidence and develop their skills. Moreover, recognizing and celebrating diverse perspectives and ideas can create a more inclusive and participatory classroom environment.

Adaptability is key in implementing strategies for increasing student participation. Educators must be willing to assess and adjust their approaches based on the needs and dynamics of their classroom. Regularly soliciting feedback from students can provide valuable insights into what strategies are working and what areas may need improvement. By remaining flexible and responsive, teachers can create a dynamic and evolving learning environment that continually fosters student participation.

In summary, increasing student participation requires a multifaceted approach that considers the diverse needs and preferences of students. By creating a supportive environment, varying instructional methods, employing active learning techniques, differentiating instruction, using effective questioning, providing student-led opportunities, and offering feedback and recognition, educators can encourage meaningful participation in the classroom. Through thoughtful planning and a commitment to continuous improvement, teachers can foster an engaging and participatory learning experience that empowers students to take an active role in their education.

Social Media and Peer Learning Networks

In the digital age, social media and peer learning networks have emerged as powerful tools for education, offering unique opportunities for collaboration, resource sharing, and community building. By leveraging these platforms, educators and students alike can engage in vibrant learning communities that transcend the confines of traditional classrooms. This chapter explores the potential of social media and peer learning networks to enhance educational experiences, providing practical advice for beginners eager to tap into these dynamic resources.

Imagine a classroom without walls, where learning extends beyond textbooks and lectures, and students connect with peers worldwide. This is the reality that social media and peer learning networks can create. Platforms such as Twitter, Facebook, Instagram, and LinkedIn facilitate the exchange of ideas and resources, allowing educators and students to engage in meaningful discussions and expand their knowledge horizons. By participating in these online communities, learners can access a wealth of information, diverse perspectives, and innovative teaching strategies.

Social media platforms offer numerous benefits for educators seeking to enhance their teaching practices and professional development. Educational hashtags on Twitter, for instance, serve as virtual meeting places where educators can share insights, ask questions, and connect with like-minded professionals. By following hashtags related to their subject area or educational interests, teachers can stay updated on the latest trends, research, and best practices. Additionally, Twitter chats provide an interactive forum for educators to engage in real-time discussions on specific topics, fostering a sense of community and collaboration.

Facebook groups dedicated to education offer a supportive space for teachers to network, share resources, and seek advice. These groups often focus on specific subjects, grade levels, or teaching methodologies, allowing educators to connect with peers who share similar interests and challenges. By participating in these groups, teachers can gain valuable insights, discover new teaching tools, and find inspiration for their classroom activities. Moreover, the collaborative nature of these groups encourages members to contribute their knowledge and expertise, enriching the collective learning experience.

Instagram, traditionally known for its visual content, has become a valuable platform for educators to share classroom activities, creative projects, and teaching tips. By following educational accounts and using relevant hashtags, teachers can discover innovative ideas and approaches to engage their students. Instagram stories and reels provide a dynamic way to showcase classroom experiences, share quick tips, and connect with a global audience. This visual storytelling aspect can inspire educators to explore new ways of presenting information and fostering student engagement.

LinkedIn, a professional networking platform, offers educators a space to connect with colleagues, join professional groups, and participate in discussions related to education. By building a professional network on LinkedIn, teachers can access job opportunities, collaborate on research projects, and gain insights into educational leadership and policy. LinkedIn articles and posts provide a platform for educators to share their expertise and contribute to the broader educational discourse, positioning themselves as thought leaders in their field.

Peer learning networks, facilitated by social media platforms, enable students to engage in collaborative learning experiences and build connections with peers beyond their immediate environment. Online study groups, discussion forums, and collaborative projects allow students to share knowledge, explore diverse perspectives, and develop critical thinking skills. By participating in peer learning networks, students can enhance their understanding of complex topics, receive feedback on their work, and gain exposure to different cultures and viewpoints.

One of the key advantages of social media and peer learning networks is their ability to provide access to a vast array of resources and expertise. Educators and students can tap into online libraries, educational websites, and open-access journals to supplement their learning. Webinar series, podcasts, and video tutorials offer additional opportunities for professional development and skill building. By curating a personalized learning network, individuals can tailor their educational experiences to align with their interests and goals.

While the benefits of social media and peer learning networks are substantial, it's important to navigate these platforms mindfully and responsibly. Digital literacy and online etiquette are essential skills for both educators and students to develop. Understanding how to evaluate the credibility of online information, protect personal privacy, and engage respectfully in online discussions are crucial aspects of participating in digital learning communities. Educators can play a vital role in guiding students to become responsible digital citizens, equipping them with the skills needed to navigate the complexities of the online world.

To effectively integrate social media and peer learning networks into educational practices, educators should set clear objectives and establish guidelines for participation. This might involve defining the purpose of using these platforms, selecting appropriate tools, and outlining expectations for online behavior. By establishing a structured framework, educators can ensure that social media and peer learning networks enhance, rather than distract from, the learning experience.

Incorporating social media and peer learning networks into education requires a balance between online and offline interactions. While digital platforms offer valuable opportunities for collaboration and resource sharing, face-to-face interactions remain essential for building strong relationships and fostering a sense of community. Educators should consider blending online and offline activities to create a holistic and engaging learning experience that leverages the strengths of both environments.

Social media and peer learning networks have the potential to transform education by creating dynamic and interconnected learning communities. By harnessing the power of these platforms, educators and students can engage in rich and meaningful learning experiences that transcend geographical boundaries and traditional educational structures. With thoughtful implementation and a commitment to digital literacy, social media and peer learning networks can serve as catalysts for innovation, collaboration, and lifelong learning in the educational landscape.

Encouraging Critical Thinking and Creativity

Fostering critical thinking and creativity in the classroom is essential for preparing students to navigate an increasingly complex and rapidly changing world. These skills empower learners to analyze information, solve problems innovatively, and approach challenges with an open mind. By encouraging critical thinking and creativity, educators can cultivate a learning environment that inspires curiosity, supports exploration, and nurtures a lifelong love of learning.

Consider a classroom buzzing with energy, where students eagerly delve into discussions, challenge assumptions, and explore new ideas. This vibrant atmosphere is the result of intentional efforts to promote critical thinking and creativity. To create such an environment, educators must employ a variety of strategies that invite students to question, experiment, and reflect.

One effective way to encourage critical thinking is by posing open-ended questions that require students to analyze, synthesize, and evaluate information. Instead of asking questions with straightforward answers, challenge students with inquiries that provoke deeper thought and exploration. For example, instead of asking, "What happened in the story?" consider asking, "Why do you think the character made that choice, and what would you have done differently?" Such questions prompt students to consider multiple perspectives, draw connections, and engage in thoughtful reflection.

Project-based learning is another powerful approach for cultivating critical thinking and creativity. By engaging in projects that require research, problem-solving, and collaboration, students have the opportunity to apply their knowledge in meaningful contexts. These projects encourage learners to take ownership of their learning, explore their interests, and develop innovative solutions. For instance, a science project might involve designing a sustainable solution to a local environmental issue, requiring students to research, experiment, and present their findings.

Encouraging creativity involves providing students with opportunities to express themselves in diverse ways. Incorporating art, music, drama, and creative writing into the curriculum allows students to explore their imagination and develop their unique voice. By valuing and celebrating diverse forms of expression, educators can create an inclusive environment where all students feel empowered to share their ideas. Offering choices in how students demonstrate their understanding, such as through multimedia presentations, artistic projects, or written reflections, can also enhance creativity and engagement.

Cultivating a growth mindset is crucial for fostering critical thinking and creativity. When students believe that their abilities can be developed through effort and persistence, they are more likely to take risks, embrace challenges, and learn from mistakes. Educators can promote a growth mindset by praising effort rather than innate ability, encouraging students to view failures as opportunities for growth, and modeling resilience in the face of challenges. By creating a classroom culture that values learning over perfection, teachers can inspire students to explore new ideas and push the boundaries of their creativity.

Collaboration is a key element in nurturing critical thinking and creativity. Working with peers allows students to exchange ideas, build on each other's strengths, and develop teamwork skills. Collaborative activities, such as group discussions, peer reviews, and team projects, provide opportunities for students to engage in meaningful dialogue, challenge assumptions, and learn from diverse perspectives. By fostering a collaborative environment, educators can create a sense of community where students feel supported and inspired to think critically and creatively.

Exposure to diverse perspectives and experiences can also enhance critical thinking and creativity. Encouraging students to explore topics from multiple viewpoints, engage with diverse cultures, and question established norms can broaden their understanding and inspire innovative thinking. Guest speakers, cultural events, and interdisciplinary projects offer valuable opportunities for students to expand their horizons and develop a more nuanced perspective on the world.

Reflective practices, such as journaling, self-assessment, and peer feedback, play an important role in promoting critical thinking and creativity. By reflecting on their learning experiences, students can deepen their understanding, identify areas for growth, and set goals for improvement. Encouraging students to regularly assess their progress and articulate their learning journey can foster self-awareness and empower them to take an active role in their education.

Integrating technology thoughtfully can also support the development of critical thinking and creativity. Digital tools and platforms offer opportunities for students to engage with interactive content, collaborate with peers worldwide, and access a wealth of resources. Virtual simulations, coding projects, and digital storytelling are just a few examples of how technology can be used to enhance critical thinking and creativity. By leveraging technology as a tool for exploration and expression, educators can create dynamic and engaging learning experiences that inspire students to think critically and creatively.

Ultimately, encouraging critical thinking and creativity requires a commitment to creating a learning environment that celebrates curiosity, values exploration, and supports diverse forms of expression. By employing a variety of strategies, from open-ended questioning and project-based learning to collaboration and reflective practices, educators can empower students to develop the skills and mindset needed to thrive in an ever-evolving world. Through intentional efforts and a focus on continuous growth, teachers can inspire the next generation of thinkers and creators to approach challenges with confidence, curiosity, and creativity.

Tools for Collaborative Learning Projects

Collaborative learning projects are an integral part of modern education, offering students the opportunity to work together, share diverse perspectives, and develop essential skills for the future workplace. The effectiveness of these projects often hinges on the tools used to facilitate communication, organization, and collaboration among participants. With the right tools, educators can create a seamless and engaging collaborative experience that enhances learning outcomes. This chapter explores a range of tools that can be employed to support collaborative learning projects, providing practical guidance for beginners seeking to integrate these resources into their teaching practice.

Envision a classroom buzzing with activity, where students are huddled together, exchanging ideas, and working towards a common goal. This dynamic environment is the essence of collaborative learning, where the synergy of group efforts leads to creative solutions and shared understanding. To harness the full potential of collaborative learning, educators must select tools that enhance communication, streamline project management, and facilitate resource sharing.

Communication is the cornerstone of any successful collaborative project, and selecting the right tools is essential for fostering effective dialogue among students. Platforms that offer instant messaging, video conferencing, and discussion forums enable students to communicate in real-time, whether they are working together in the same room or across different locations. Tools like Zoom, Microsoft Teams, and Google Meet provide reliable options for video conferencing, allowing students to hold virtual meetings, present their ideas, and engage in lively discussions. These platforms also offer features such as screen sharing and breakout rooms, which enhance collaboration by enabling students to work in smaller groups or share their work with the entire class.

For text-based communication, platforms like Slack and Microsoft Teams offer a structured approach to conversations, with channels dedicated to specific topics or projects. These tools allow students to organize discussions, share files, and integrate with other applications, creating a centralized hub for all project-related communication. By providing a space for asynchronous communication, these platforms accommodate different schedules and time zones, ensuring that all students can participate and contribute at their convenience.

Organization and project management are critical components of collaborative learning projects, and tools that facilitate these processes can greatly enhance productivity and efficiency. Project management platforms like Trello and Asana offer visual interfaces that help students plan, track, and manage their tasks. By creating boards, lists, and cards, students can outline project milestones, assign responsibilities, and monitor progress. These tools also allow for the integration of deadlines, checklists, and attachments, providing a comprehensive overview of the project's status and ensuring that all team members are aligned and informed.

Resource sharing is another key element of collaborative projects, and cloud-based storage solutions like Google Drive, Dropbox, and OneDrive offer reliable options for storing and sharing files. These platforms enable students to access documents, presentations, and multimedia resources from any device, ensuring that all team members have the information they need at their fingertips. Collaborative editing features, such as those offered by Google Docs and Microsoft Office 365, allow students to work simultaneously on documents, spreadsheets, and presentations, facilitating real-time collaboration and feedback.

Creativity and innovation are important aspects of collaborative learning, and tools that support these elements can inspire students to explore new ideas and approaches. Digital whiteboards like Miro and Jamboard offer interactive canvases where students can brainstorm, sketch, and organize their thoughts visually. These tools support creativity by allowing students to collaborate on mind maps, storyboards, and design thinking exercises, fostering an environment of experimentation and exploration.

Assessment and feedback are essential for the success of collaborative projects, and tools that facilitate these processes can support both educators and students. Platforms like Padlet and Flipgrid offer options for sharing student work and receiving feedback from peers and instructors. These tools enable students to present their ideas, reflect on their learning experiences, and engage in constructive dialogue with their peers. By creating a space for feedback and reflection, educators can support continuous improvement and encourage students to take ownership of their learning journey.

While the selection of tools is important, the successful implementation of collaborative learning projects also requires thoughtful planning and facilitation. Educators should consider the specific needs and preferences of their students, as well as the goals and objectives of the project, when choosing tools. Providing clear instructions, guidelines, and support for using these tools can help students feel confident and capable in navigating the digital landscape.

Additionally, fostering a culture of collaboration and mutual respect is crucial for the success of any collaborative project. Encouraging students to communicate openly, listen actively, and value diverse perspectives can create a positive and inclusive environment where all team members feel empowered to contribute. By modeling collaborative behaviors and providing opportunities for team-building activities, educators can nurture a sense of community and shared purpose among their students.

In conclusion, the use of tools for collaborative learning projects can greatly enhance the educational experience by facilitating communication, organization, creativity, and assessment. By thoughtfully selecting and integrating these tools, educators can create dynamic and engaging learning environments that prepare students for the collaborative challenges of the future. Through careful planning, support, and a commitment to fostering a collaborative culture, teachers can empower their students to work together, think critically, and innovate, ultimately leading to richer and more meaningful learning outcomes

Measuring and Assessing Student Engagement

Student engagement is a cornerstone of effective education, reflecting the level of interest, curiosity, and participation that students bring to their learning experiences. Measuring and assessing this engagement can provide valuable insights into students' academic progress and overall well-being, allowing educators to tailor their teaching strategies to better meet the needs of their learners. This chapter delves into the methods and tools available to gauge student engagement, offering practical advice for educators seeking to enhance their assessment practices.

Imagine a classroom where students are not only present but fully immersed in their learning. They ask questions, contribute to discussions, and eagerly dive into activities. This type of engagement is not only desirable but also measurable. By understanding and assessing student engagement, educators can identify areas of strength and opportunities for growth, ultimately fostering a more dynamic and supportive learning environment.

One of the first steps in measuring student engagement is to recognize its multifaceted nature. Engagement can be understood through three primary dimensions: behavioral, emotional, and cognitive. Behavioral engagement refers to students' participation in academic and extracurricular activities, including attendance, homework completion, and involvement in class discussions. Emotional engagement encompasses students' feelings towards school, teachers, and peers, reflecting their sense of belonging and motivation. Cognitive engagement involves the investment of effort in learning, characterized by the use of deep learning strategies and a willingness to tackle challenging tasks.

To effectively assess these dimensions, educators can employ a variety of methods, both qualitative and quantitative. Observations, for instance, provide a rich source of qualitative data, allowing teachers to gather insights into students' behaviors and interactions in the classroom. By paying close attention to how students participate in activities, respond to questions, and interact with peers, educators can gain a deeper understanding of their engagement levels. Taking detailed notes during observations and reflecting on patterns can help identify trends and inform instructional decisions.

Surveys and questionnaires offer a quantitative approach to measuring student engagement, providing structured data that can be analyzed and compared over time. These tools can be designed to capture students' self-reported levels of engagement, motivation, and attitudes towards learning. Questions might address topics such as students' interest in the subject matter, their sense of belonging in the classroom, and their use of study strategies. By administering surveys periodically, educators can track changes in engagement and identify factors that may influence it.

Student interviews and focus groups offer an opportunity for in-depth exploration of engagement, allowing educators to gather qualitative insights directly from students. Through open-ended questions and guided discussions, students can share their perspectives on what motivates them, the challenges they face, and the aspects of learning they find most engaging. These conversations can reveal valuable information about students' experiences and preferences, helping educators tailor their teaching approaches to better support engagement.

In addition to direct measures of engagement, educators can explore indirect indicators, such as academic performance, attendance records, and classroom behavior. While these indicators may not provide a complete picture of engagement, they can offer valuable context and highlight areas that may require further investigation. For instance, a sudden drop in attendance or a decline in academic performance may signal disengagement, prompting educators to explore underlying causes and implement targeted interventions.

Technology offers innovative tools for assessing student engagement, enabling educators to gather data in real-time and access a wealth of analytics. Learning management systems (LMS) and educational apps often include features that track students' interactions with course materials, such as time spent on assignments, participation in online discussions, and completion of quizzes. By analyzing this data, educators can gain insights into students' engagement patterns and identify opportunities for intervention and support.

While measuring and assessing student engagement is valuable, it is essential to approach the process with sensitivity and respect for students' individuality. Engagement is a personal and dynamic experience, influenced by a range of factors, including cultural background, personal interests, and external circumstances. Educators should strive to create an inclusive and supportive environment that acknowledges and values these differences, fostering a sense of belonging and empowerment for all students.

Feedback plays a crucial role in the assessment process, providing students with valuable insights into their engagement and learning progress. By offering constructive and timely feedback, educators can guide students in reflecting on their engagement levels and setting goals for improvement. Encouraging students to provide feedback on their learning experiences can also empower them to take an active role in shaping their educational journey, fostering a sense of ownership and agency.

Ultimately, measuring and assessing student engagement requires a holistic and flexible approach, integrating a range of methods and tools to capture the complexity of the engagement experience. By thoughtfully selecting and combining these approaches, educators can gain a comprehensive understanding of student engagement and use this information to enhance their teaching practices. Through ongoing reflection, collaboration, and a commitment to continuous improvement, teachers can create a learning environment where all students feel motivated, supported, and engaged in their pursuit of knowledge.